Student Stress
at the Transition to Middle School

Norton Books in Education

Student Stress at the Transition to Middle School

An A-to-Z Guide
for Implementing an Emotional Health Checkup

Ann Vander Stoep
and
Kelly Thompson

W.W. Norton & Company
Independent Publishers Since 1923
New York • London

Note to Readers: Models and/or techniques described in this volume are illustrative or are included for general informational purposes only; neither the publisher nor the author(s) can guarantee the efficacy or appropriateness of any particular recommendation in every circumstance.

For information about permission to reproduce selections from this book, write to Permissions, W. W. Norton & Company, Inc., 500 Fifth Avenue, New York, NY 10110

For information about special discounts for bulk purchases, please contact W. W. Norton Special Sales at specialsales@wwnorton.com or 800-233-4830

Manufacturing by Edwards Brothers Malloy
Production manager: Christine Critelli

Library of Congress Cataloging-in-Publication Data

Names: Vander Stoep, Ann. | Thompson, Kelly, 1966-
Title: Student stress at the transition to middle school : an A-to-Z guide for implementing an emotional health checkup / Ann Vander Stoep and Kelly Thompson.
Description: New York : W. W Norton & Company, 2016. | Series: Norton books in education | Includes bibliographical references and index.
Identifiers: LCCN 2016013584 | ISBN 9780393709865 (pbk.)
Subjects: LCSH: School children—Mental health services. | Middle school students.
Classification: LCC LB3013.4 .V36 2016 | DDC 371.7/13—dc23 LC record available at http://lccn.loc.gov/2016013584

W. W. Norton & Company, Inc.
500 Fifth Avenue, New York, N.Y. 10110
www.wwnorton.com

W. W. Norton & Company Ltd.
15 Carlisle Street, London W1D 3BS

1 2 3 4 5 6 7 8 9 0

For Jim, a genuine champion

Contents

Acknowledgments

There are so many to thank for generously supporting us on our journey to write this book. Fourteen years ago, as we screened students in Aki Kurose Middle School classrooms, we never suspected that one day we would be writing a book about our middle school adventures.

We want to thank our friend, colleague and co-developer, Elizabeth McCauley, whose heart and mind are woven into the Emotional Health Checkup (EHC) and this book. Elizabeth is a developmental and clinical psychologist, a professor at the University of Washington, and the associate director of the Department of Child and Adolescent Psychiatry and Behavioral Health at Seattle Children's.

We are blessed to count many dedicated educators among our friends and family. Our sisters, Johanna Vander Stoep, retired K–8 teacher and principal, and Kathryn Thompson, a veteran special education teacher, offered thoughtful advice and sisterly support. It was good to have reality checks from retired high school teacher Joan Horn, retired K–6 counselor Mary Jackson, retired sixth grade teacher Kasey Jeffers, and Carolyn Grigsby, who is still busy teaching elementary students in California.

Our artist, Mesa Schumacher, is a gem who worked skillfully, amiably, patiently, and diplomatically with our differing artistic sensibilities to create a blend of images that we found just right. Our friend and colleague, Kathleen Myers, child and adolescent psychiatrist, read with great care and offered clear, invaluable critiques.

We wish to give special acknowledgment to BiHoa Caldwell, who served competently and compassionately as a principal for 21 years in the Seattle Public Schools. BiHoa was the principal at Aki Kurose Middle School for 10 years and was our first EHC champion. We have learned so much from many Seattle public school teachers, counselors, principals, and students. Their stories populate the pages of this book. Over the years, we have had the good fortune to work with dozens of capable classroom screeners and skilled EHC counselors, and we offer them our heartfelt thanks.

Several young readers who are members of our University of Washington research team contributed excellent editing and formatting help. We could not have gone to print without Stephanie Violante, Shanon Cox, and Alexis Torres-Dawson. And where would we be without ongoing support from our colleague Nancy Namkung? Nowhere, to be sure.

We are grateful to our editing team. Deborah Malmud, vice president at W. W. Norton and director of Norton Professional Books, originally approached us to write this handbook, having read about the Emotional Health Checkup in the scientific literature. Deborah had a wonderful vision and guided us with patience and grace. Her colleagues Elizabeth Baird and Alison Lewis were knowledgeable and unflappable.

From 2001 to 2005 we received federal support from the National Institute of Mental Health (R01

MH63711) that enabled us to develop and implement the EHC. Seattle philanthropists, Don and JoEllen Loeb, helped to fund EHC implementation and evaluation in the Seattle Public Schools from 2006 to 2009. We are very grateful for their support and hope that in carrying out the EHC other school districts will have the good fortune of working with visionary, enthusiastic, and generous community members.

Kelly gives a special shout-out to Mike Schumacher, her companion and supporter in every way. She is impressed and inspired every day by her next generation: Mesa, Austin, Logan, Cooper, and Jade.

Ann has been inspired and encouraged by four generations of family members. Ann's parents, Suzi and Jim Vander Stoep, thrived in small-town public schools in Washington state, as did Ann and her siblings, Johanna and J. Having been Seattle public school students for a combined total of 43 person-years, Ann's kids and grandkids, Brook, Roxie Jane, Jack, and Marley Mae, have broadened her appreciation for the wonderful things that happen in public school communities.

Introduction

Each fall, children begin middle school with a mix of excitement and trepidation. Middle school students face many changes and can easily get stressed out as they transition into a new and unfamiliar setting. Getting lost, memorizing locker combinations, and meeting new academic demands can cause stress. Students have to make adjustments to new rules, changing clothes for gym, and early morning bus rides. They are worried about grades, bullies, and pressure from older students to try drugs or alcohol. By mid-fall, most students have managed the stress associated with the transition and have settled into new routines. However, an estimated 15% of students become overwhelmed by the new academic and social demands.

The words "stress" and "distress" are often used interchangeably, but they are two different things. When middle school students are unable to manage stress, they become distressed. Stress is the feeling of being under pressure and is related to the events or activities of daily living. Distress results from prolonged exposure to stress and manifests in symptoms such as intestinal problems, headaches, trouble sleeping, and fatigue. Distress is difficult to detect, and many students who suffer do so silently. This is a problem. If we don't know when students are suffering, we can't address their needs. Left unaddressed, distress can grow into depression, school failure, or problem substance use.

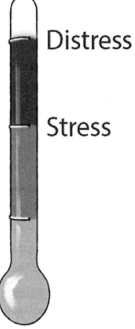

The Emotional Health Checkup (EHC) is a school-based early detection and response program. It encourages a unique partnership between schools, parents, and students to tackle problems that interfere with a healthy adjustment during this exciting and challenging time of life. The goal of the EHC is to identify and support distressed students who are at risk of falling behind during their transition to middle school. Students in need are linked to support—people, services, and activities that will help them get on track for success in middle school.

We first implemented the EHC in 2001 at Aki Kurose Middle School in the Seattle Public Schools. Ann Vander Stoep, a public mental health practitioner, and Elizabeth McCauley, a clinical psychologist, had worked in the district for many years. Based at the University of Washington, they had observed how adolescents were vulnerable to distress during transitions to middle school, high school, and adulthood.

In the fall of 2001, Ann and Elizabeth launched a new research project. They approached BiHoa

Caldwell, the principal at Aki Kurose Middle School. Aki Kurose was considered a high-need school, where 85% of students qualified for free or reduced-price lunch, and many students had parents who were first-generation immigrants. The research plan was to review academic and disciplinary records to identify middle school students at risk for depression. BiHoa felt that a review of school records would miss many distressed students. She wanted to find a more comprehensive approach for detecting distress and also requested that all distressed students be followed up to address their concerns. She did not want any students to fall through the cracks.

In response to BiHoa's request, Ann and Elizabeth designed the EHC. During the first year, the EHC team administered screening questionnaires to 246 students in Aki Kurose homeroom classes. Kelly Thompson, an experienced clinical social worker, joined the team to help conduct assessments of the 80 students who showed signs of distress.

During the next decade, we implemented the EHC in a number of Seattle middle schools. Over 5,000 students participated. Approximately 750 students took part in follow-up assessments, and of those, 450 were determined to need support. A review of the program revealed that after these students and their parents worked with an EHC counselor to develop a Support Plan, three quarters of them had been linked to the recommended support within two weeks.

The EHC design incorporates a practical approach for linking students to both formal and informal support. Academic concerns are addressed with solutions like homework clubs, tutors, or asking a parent to set up a quiet space for doing homework. Students with social concerns are linked to activities such as sports teams and social skills groups or are encouraged to connect with friends on weekends. Emotional concerns are addressed through referrals to counseling support or fostering closer connections with a parent, relative, or friend.

Over the years, we evaluated and modified the EHC. Implementation and quality improvement efforts were supported with funding from interested federal agencies and enthusiastic local donors. The result of these efforts is a simple, straightforward, public health approach to addressing emotional health needs of students who are making the transition to middle school.

This handbook offers step-by-step assistance to school personnel, parents, or other interested community members who want to learn about and potentially implement the program. The handbook has two parts. The goal of Part I is to answer the question, "Why implement the EHC?" Readers are introduced to the four core EHC activities:

1. Universal classroom screening
2. Following up with students who show signs of distress

3. Formulating a Student Support Plan
4. Connecting with parents* during a Parent Phone Call

Then readers learn what they need to know to make an informed decision about whether the EHC is a good fit for their school.

Part II is an A-to-Z guide to implementing the EHC. Detailed information is presented on how to introduce the program to parents and students, obtain parent permission, and implement the four core activities. Training agendas, scripts, and organizational materials are included. Part II concludes with suggestions for how the program could be adapted to address other problems and circumstances and an EHC wrap-up.

The transition to middle school can be a stressful time for young adolescents. We believe that taking early action to detect and address distress is good for students, parents, and schools and hope this book inspires you.

---

* A note about language. While we appreciate the many adults who are primary caregivers and guardians of middle school students, for ease in reading, we use the single term "parent" to denote all caregivers.

Part I

Student Stress
at the Transition to Middle School

Chapter 1

It's a Big Deal:
Emotional Health in Middle School

The Transition to Middle School

Summer is over. It is the start of another school year. Students who are making the transition from elementary to middle school are excited and apprehensive. They are feeling grown up, looking forward to seeing old friends, and eager to make a fresh start in a new school. But do not be fooled. Starting middle school can also be stressful. Middle school students are exploring a variety of interests. They want to fit in and worry about being judged or teased. With the onset of puberty, they are entering a period of rapid physical growth. It is a time of high energy as well as frequent fatigue. They turn less often to parents for ideas and affirmation and rely more on peers for advice, validation, and support. Many who were comfortable with the routines and expectations of elementary school enter middle school with a feeling of unease and loss of self-confidence. According to a 2015 survey of students transitioning to middle school, undressing in front of others for gym class was the top concern, followed by taking more difficult classes, taking tests, using a locker, getting lost, being pressured by peers to drink and smoke, being bullied, and meeting academic challenges (Bailey, Giles, & Rogers, 2015; Akos, 2002).

> I thought the older kids would pick on us like in the movies. I got a sick feeling when I walked into school every morning.—Maria
>
> I was worried there was going to be tons of homework.—LaToya
>
> My family can't afford new clothes. I hate how I look.—James

Things are changing. Middle school students encounter many changes associated with their new school setting and daily schedule.

- Small, familiar elementary schools are a thing of the past. Middle schools are large and hard to navigate.

- School starts early in the morning, even though adolescent biological clocks are beginning to shift in the direction of staying up later and needing more daytime sleep (Carskadon, 2011).

- Middle schools are often located a long distance from home. Students who walked to elementary school may now ride a bus for the first time.

- Students change classes every hour.

- To get to classes on time, students cope with crowded, busy hallways during brief passing periods.

- Students are assigned a locker and need to remember where it is, how to use the combination, and how to manage books, folders, and school supplies.

- No more recess.

Things are changing. Social relationships and expectations are changing and more demanding.

- Students who were confident in elementary school are now the youngest kids in the building and aware they have lots to learn.

- Middle school students have five or six teachers with different personalities, rules, and expectations.

- Academic demands accelerate. Students have more homework and may be receiving grades for the first time.

- Students miss friends who attend different schools or have different class schedules.

- Middle school students go through puberty at different rates. Both the slower- and faster-maturing students may feel awkward.

- In gym class, students are expected to change clothes in front of their peers.

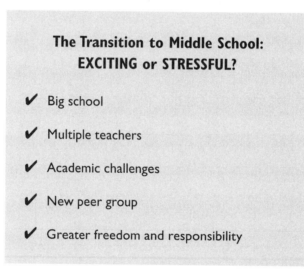

**The Transition to Middle School:
EXCITING or STRESSFUL?**

✔ Big school

✔ Multiple teachers

✔ Academic challenges

✔ New peer group

✔ Greater freedom and responsibility

There is a lot at stake. Hard to believe, but these young adolescents are at a major turning point. How they perform in the next few years will affect their future educational and vocational paths. Research conducted in Chicago and Philadelphia supports the idea that successful school transitions are critical. Failing a course in the first year of high school and even the first year of middle school are both strong predictors that a student will not graduate from high school on time (Balfanz, Herzog, & Mac Iver, 2007; Neild & Balfanz, 2006; Roderick, 2003). Thus, a successful transition from elementary school to middle school forms a foundation for success in high school and beyond.

Stress

The changes students face during their transition to middle school can be stressful. Stress is the feeling of being under mental, physical, or emotional pressure and is caused by exposure to events or activities that are stressors. A fact sheet from the National Institute of Mental Health (n.d.) describes three different types of stressors:

- Routine stressors include the typical pressures of school, family, peers, and other daily responsibilities.

- Sudden change stressors include abrupt or difficult changes such as illness, loss of a loved one, or divorce.

- Traumatic stressors are events, like major accidents, natural disasters, or abuse, in which a person may be seriously hurt or in danger of being killed.

Stress affects everyone, but individuals have different ways of reacting to stressors. A stressful situation that feels unpleasant to one person can be invigorating to someone else. Some students experience their first middle school quiz as a scary unknown that causes them to lose sleep, while others feel confident and excited to demonstrate their new knowledge and skills.

Scientists have demonstrated that exposure to mild stressors can activate and strengthen parts of the brain that enable a student to weigh options and make reasoned decisions (Vohs & Baumeister, 2011; Dahl, 2004; Steinberg et al., 2006). Accelerated academic demands, for example, are stressors that present students with opportunities to develop new problem-solving skills. With increased homework loads and more rigorous testing, students hone their study habits, learn to manage their time, turn to friends and family members for help, and ask teachers for clarification when they don't understand a concept. They feel accomplished when they manage the varying expectations of different teachers, turn in their homework on time, and pass their exams. When students respond to stressors and experience positive outcomes, it promotes brain maturation and increases confidence in facing the next stressor (Katz et al., 2009).

Sometimes, particularly when students are exposed to a sudden change or traumatic stressor, different parts of the brain are activated that cause them to act without considering options or anticipating consequences. Responses such as skipping class to avoid a test, getting edgy or defiant with teachers, or attending to social media while studying can have negative consequences in the short term and over the longer term as well. Inadequate responses to stress eventually produce more stress, resulting in a negative emotional state called distress (Hertzman & Boyce, 2010).

Distress can develop for many reasons but, in general, results from prolonged exposure to a stressor combined with an inadequate stress response. Distress may also result when there are multiple stressors or if a stressor is so intense that the usual stress response is insufficient in helping a person cope effectively. When stress gives way to distress, it can take a big toll emotionally and physically, affecting how a person feels, thinks, and behaves (Lupien, McEwaen, Gunnar, & Heim, 2009). Bodies respond differently, but people experiencing distress suffer. Some individuals will experience symptoms in their digestive or immune systems. Some can't sleep. Some complain of aches and pains and get physically run down, while others experience the sensation of being stuck, worried, or discouraged. Here are some warning signs that can indicate an adolescent is distressed (Mondimore, 2002):

1. Frequent headaches or gastrointestinal upset
2. Irritability and anger outbursts
3. Poor concentration
4. Increased levels of anxiety or sadness
5. Sleep problems
6. Overeating or lack of appetite
7. Social withdrawal
8. Lack of motivation

Stress Takes a Toll on Middle School Students

Differences in stress exposure, brain development, and social support translate into tremendous variability in adolescent distress. As they transition into middle school, students vary widely in their exposure to routine, sudden change and traumatic stressors. Their brains are maturing at different rates, affecting whether they are able to make thoughtful decisions in the midst of stressful situations. The strength of their support networks vary widely.

When distressed, a student gets distracted, feels fatigued, and has a hard time making decisions (Diamond, 2010). Learning and academic achievement are compromised. One of the unfortunate consequences of distress is that it can cause feelings of hopelessness and diminish the motivation and confidence a student needs to engage socially with peers or to connect with adults who could offer support.

Early identification of distressed adolescents can prompt intervention that gets them back on track and prevents progression to more serious emotional health conditions. Helping students recognize when they are distressed and learn coping strategies that produce positive outcomes can greatly improve both their emotional and physical well-being and their academic performance. Ideally, during middle school all students will develop the skills, support, and confidence they need to cope effectively with stressors, so that challenges provide stepping stones toward positive emotional health. On the other hand, when skills, support, and confidence are inadequate to buffer stress, emotional health suffers.

The transition to middle school coincides with a dramatic upturn in the incidence of serious emotional health problems, including depression, anxiety, and substance abuse (Steinberg et al., 2006). These problems are debilitating and often persist into the adult years. An estimated one in five youths in the United States experiences a diagnosable and functionally impairing mental health disorder (Merikangas et al., 2010). Another one in five has signs of emotional distress that do not meet full criteria for a diagnosis. In a study conducted in public schools in the state of Oregon, 20% of the adolescents reported they had suffered an episode of clinical depression by the age of 18 (Lewinsohn, Rohde, & Seeley, 1998).

While emotional health problems are common among adolescents, less than a quarter of adolescents with these problems receive treatment (Merikangas et al., 2010, 2011). Interestingly, adolescents who do access treatment are more likely to get it at school than in health care or other settings (Farmer, Burns, Phillips, Angold, & Costello, 2003; Chatterji, Caffray, Crowe, Freeman, & Jensen, 2004; Langer et al., 2015).

Suffering in Silence

Unlike a broken arm or a runny nose, distress is a condition that can be difficult for others to see with the naked eye. Many distressed students suffer silently. It can be hard to identify students who are having trouble concentrating in class, not sleeping at night, or feeling badly about themselves. Students struggle with very difficult feelings in very quiet ways. The silent suffering associated with distress is problematic because it cannot be addressed unless it can be detected.

As students move from elementary to middle school, detecting their distress gets more challenging. Elementary school teachers have close contact with a small number of students. They typically interact with 20–23 students (U.S. Department of Education, 2011), 4–6 hours every day, which provides them with more opportunities to identify and address student problems. Parents of children in elementary school generally have more access to what students are experiencing and feeling. Their children are apt to come to them with both skinned knees and bruised feelings. Many parents volunteer in classrooms or see teachers at the start or end of the school day. They typically know the parents of their child's playmates. Because parents of elementary school students observe and talk with their children on a regular basis, if something is amiss, they tend to be aware it.

Once students reach middle school, they undergo less adult scrutiny (Steinberg et al., 2006). Accordingly, their distress is more likely to go unnoticed. Middle school teachers have a new roster of students each period, and thus have less time to get to know their students individually. Teachers may not have enough information about past academic performance to know which students are performing up to their potential. Teachers and parents communicate less frequently than in elementary school. Parents do not see report cards or attend parent-teacher conferences until late in the fall. Middle school students are more independent and communicate less frequently with their parents and other adults. They are often reluctant to have their parents involved at school. At a time when stress is heightened, adult oversight diminishes, leaving middle school students vulnerable to distress.

A Program to Detect and Address Distress

The Emotional Health Checkup (EHC) is a three-part program designed to identify and address the emotional health needs of students as they transition to middle school (Vander Stoep et al., 2005). The first part of the EHC is a screening. A screening team administers a questionnaire to all incoming middle school students. In the second part of the EHC, students who show signs of distress on the questionnaire meet with an EHC counselor for a Student Check-In. The Check-In is a structured conversation designed to evaluate the source of the student's distress and to generate ideas for addressing concerns. The Check-In concludes with the development of a Support Plan for students who need a helping hand. In the third part of the EHC, the counselor calls a parent to discuss the child's middle school transition and the Support Plan. The program aims to check up on the emotional health needs of all students at a critical developmental transition.

The "Go Out and Get 'Em" Approach

Most emotional health programs for youths operate on a come-and-get-it basis. Health care providers in school or community clinics wait for youths to come to them. To access services, even those provided at school, a student needs to find out what is available and then set up an appointment with a provider. For many reasons, the come-and-get-it approach is insufficient when the goal is to detect and address emotional health needs. First, since distress is hard to detect, emotional health problems may go unrecognized, with the consequence that students remain disconnected from support. Even a parent or young adolescent who does recognize a need may not know where to turn for help. Some feel awkward asking for help. Others worry about being stigmatized or labeled. Still others run into barriers during the help-seeking process. For these reasons, rather than waiting for students to come and get help, the EHC uses a "go out and get 'em" approach.

Going out and getting students is consistent with the public health model. The goal of a public health program is to promote health within an entire community (CDC Foundation, n.d.). Thus, active efforts are made to reach all community members. Antismoking campaigns and routine water testing and treatment both use a public health model to improve the health of communities. Although this model is seldom applied to address children's emotional health, the school community is a good place to use a public health model.

The EHC goes out and gets 'em at each step of the way. The screening team goes into the classroom and gets an emotional health screen from all students as they enter middle school. Next, EHC counselors go out and talk with every student showing signs of distress. Finally, the program gets parents involved with helping to link students to support.

Students attending a school that implements the EHC do not have to wait for someone to recognize that they need help. They do not have to get up the nerve to ask an adult for help. Parents do not have to figure out on their own what services are available and how to access them. A parent simply has to return a signed permission form, and EHC staff go out and get the student. When the EHC ends in late fall, the school will have taken responsibility for systematically checking on the emotional health of each new student and addressing the needs of those who show signs of distress.

Chapter 2

Screening to Detect Distress

Classroom-based emotional health screening is the first step in the early detection of student distress. Screening refers to testing people for symptoms of conditions that are both (1) difficult to detect, and (2) responsive to early intervention (Morrison, 1992). An eye exam, a hearing test, or a mammogram are screening tests that can detect early warning signs and prompt further evaluation and interventions at an early stage of a problem. Early intervention helps reduce vision or hearing impairment and in the case of breast cancer, saves lives.

History of Emotional Health Screening

When everyone in a community is screened, it is called universal screening. In the United States, universal emotional health screening was first carried out as part of the routine health examination for army recruits during World War II. During World War I, many soldiers became overwhelmed and emotionally incapacitated by the stress of trench warfare (Smith & Pear, 1918). They suffered from what came to be known as shell shock. The army recognized the serious adverse effects of shell shock on the morale and functioning of soldiers and wanted to prevent its widespread effects from recurring in future military conflicts. The result was that, during World War II, emotional health screening was carried out routinely to determine eligibility for combat.

The army screened recruits with a self-report questionnaire called the Cornell Selectee Index (Weider, Mitelmann, Wechsler, Wolff, & Meixner, 1944). The index asked about symptoms of depression and anxiety because these symptoms are good predictors of general emotional health status. More recently, researchers and clinicians have turned their attention to screening children and adolescents for emotional health problems. They have found that questionnaires targeting depression work well to find cases of clinical depression and are also useful as a general screen for emotional distress (Crisan, 2014). The EHC draws on this history, using a depression questionnaire to carry out universal screening for distress in young adolescents during their transition to middle school.

Screening Adolescents for Emotional Distress

The tool used in the EHC to screen for distress is called the Mood and Feelings Questionnaire (MFQ; Angold & Costello, 1987). Public mental health researchers at Duke University developed the MFQ, and it has been administered to thousands of girls and boys aged 7 to 18 from diverse racial and economic backgrounds. The MFQ is a validated screening test for child and adolescent emotional distress (Banh et al., 2012; Kent, Vostanis, & Feehan, 1997; Burleson-Daviss et al., 2006). Validation means the MFQ has gone through extensive testing to determine that it measures what it is supposed to measure. Another way to think about the validity of the MFQ is that if a student has a high score, it is very likely that he or she is distressed. A low score means that the student is most likely not distressed. During EHC screening, students rate the MFQ items, shown below.

MOOD AND FEELINGS QUESTIONNAIRE

This form is about how you might have been feeling or acting lately.

For each question, please check how much you have felt or acted this way *in the past two weeks*.

If a sentence was true about you most of the time, check TRUE.
If a sentence was only sometimes true, check SOMETIMES.
If a sentence was not true about you, check NOT TRUE.

	TRUE	SOME TIMES	NOT TRUE
1. I felt miserable or unhappy...	☐	☐	☐
2. I didn't enjoy anything at all...	☐	☐	☐
3. I was less hungry than usual..	☐	☐	☐
4. I ate more than usual	☐	☐	☐
5. I felt so tired I just sat around and did nothing.....................	☐	☐	☐
6. I was moving and walking more slowly than usual	☐	☐	☐
7. I was very restless...	☐	☐	☐
8. I felt I was no good anymore..	☐	☐	☐
9. I blamed myself for things that weren't my fault..................	☐	☐	☐
10. It was hard for me to make up my mind............................	☐	☐	☐
11. I felt grumpy and cross with my parents............................	☐	☐	☐
12. I felt like talking less than usual......................................	☐	☐	☐
13. I was talking more slowly than usual.................................	☐	☐	☐

TURN OVER →

	TRUE	SOME TIMES	NOT TRUE
14. I cried a lot..	☐	☐	☐
15. I thought there was nothing good for me in the future...........	☐	☐	☐
16. I thought my family was better off without me.....................	☐	☐	☐
17. I didn't want to see my friends...	☐	☐	☐
18. I found it hard to think properly or concentrate...................	☐	☐	☐
19. I thought bad things would happen to me...........................	☐	☐	☐
20. I hated myself..	☐	☐	☐
21. I felt that I was a bad person...	☐	☐	☐
22. I thought I looked ugly...	☐	☐	☐
23. I worried about aches and pains.....................................	☐	☐	☐
24. I felt lonely...	☐	☐	☐
25. I thought nobody really loved me.....................................	☐	☐	☐
26. I didn't have any fun at school..	☐	☐	☐
27. I thought I would never be as good as other kids................	☐	☐	☐
28. I did everything wrong..	☐	☐	☐
29. I didn't sleep as well as I usually sleep...........................	☐	☐	☐
30. I slept a lot more than usual...	☐	☐	☐

A Positive Screening Score Is Like Running a Fever

A screening questionnaire detects distress like a thermometer detects a fever. A high temperature reading on a thermometer is an indication that a child has an illness. Likewise, a high score on the MFQ indicates that a student has an emotional health concern. High fevers and high screening scores do not provide a diagnosis. They signal a need for further evaluation. During the EHC, the MFQ is used to take the student's emotional health temperature. When the temperature is high, the student participates in the second part of the EHC, a Student Check-In to investigate the cause of the fever.

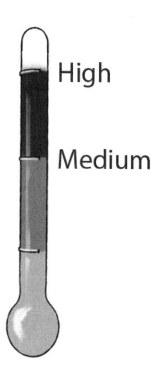

Scoring the MFQ

The MFQ is scored by assigning each item a numerical value of 2 (*true most of the time*), 1 (*sometimes true*), or 0 (*not true*), with a total possible high score of 60. The developers of the MFQ do not identify a specific cutoff score to indicate stress, distress, or depression. They caution that as with all screening tests, there is no single MFQ score that is best to use in all circumstances and recommend that users of the MFQ decide what score will be most useful in their particular situation (Costello & Angold, 1988; Angold, n.d.). For example, users wanting to identify youths who meet criteria for a diagnosis of depression use a higher cutoff score than users who want to identify youths with distress or early warning signs of depression. The EHC sets the cutoff score at 18 to indicate distress. Any score of 18 or above is considered a positive screen and signals the need for a Student Check-In. Any score below 18 is considered a negative screen.

A Note About False Positives and False Negatives

No screening test is accurate 100% of the time. There are two kinds of inaccuracies, called false positives and false negatives. When scoring the MFQ, there will be some students who score above the designated cutoff of 18 who are not truly distressed. These students are called false positives. They may have scored high because they were having a bad day on Screening Day, or they misunderstood questionnaire items. There will also be some students who are truly distressed who score below the cutoff.

These students are called false negatives. They may have scored low because they did not feel comfortable answering personal questions in the classroom setting, or they misunderstood the instructions. Although not 100% accurate, most students will score in a range consistent with their distress level. During the Check-In, a few students who are not truly distressed, false positives, will have a brief, friendly conversation with an EHC counselor. A few distressed students will be overlooked, but hopefully these false negatives will be identified later through come-and-get-it channels in place at school. Because emotional health problems like depression and anxiety have the potential to interfere with children's cognitive, emotional, and social functioning (Lima et al., 2013), screening questionnaires like the MFQ that assist in detecting early signs of distress are valuable tools for those concerned about adolescent emotional health.

Chapter 3

The EHC From Start to Finish

Doing the Numbers on the EHC

The EHC operates like a funnel, systematically sorting students several times until the ones who need extra help are identified and linked with support. The following is an illustration of how the EHC sorts students in a middle school with an incoming class of 250 students (Vander Stoep et al., 2005).

The first sorting takes place on Screening Day. When 250 students are screened, the MFQ sorts students into two groups:

1. Students who show signs of distress: Depending upon the demographic makeup of students enrolled in the middle school, 10 to 30% of the students will screen positive for distress (Kuo, Vander Stoep, McCauley, & Kernic, 2009). In the school with 250 students, approximately 50 students, or 20%, score high. The 50 students sorted into this group will get a Student Check-In.
2. Students who do not show signs of distress: 200 students, or 80%, are sorted into this group.

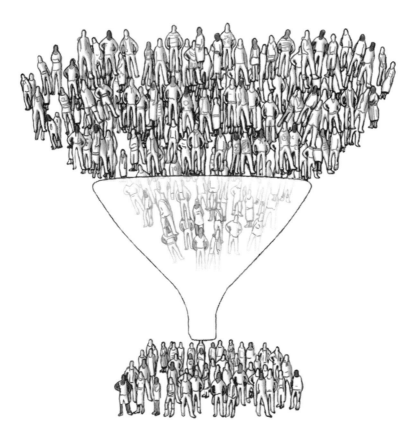

The 50 students sorted into the distress group will get a Student Check-In. The second sorting occurs during the Check-In, where the 50 distressed students are sorted into three different groups:

1. <u>Students who need a Support Plan</u>: 30 students, or 60%, need additional support.
2. <u>Students who are distressed but are already well supported</u>: 15 students, or 30%, are funneled into this group.
3. <u>Students who are not truly distressed</u>: 5 students, or 10%, are sorted into this group.

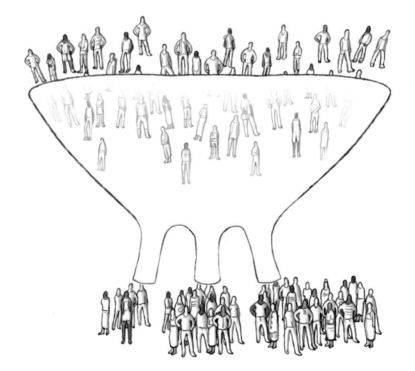

The third sorting happens with students who need a Support Plan. Support Plans target concerns related to three areas: academic, social, and emotional functioning. Although students are sorted according to their needs, plans often address more than one area of concern. Of the 30 students with Support Plans:

- Sixty percent need some form of academic support. These students are linked to homework clubs, tutoring, or homework help from family members or teachers.

- Fifty percent need more peer social support. For these students, the EHC counselor encourages social engagement through joining an after-school activity or reconnecting with old friends.

- Seventy percent need adult social or emotional support. This can prompt an introduction to the school counselor or an activation of social support from family members or neighbors.

- Ten percent are referred to mental health services at school or in the community to address more serious emotional health concerns.

The number of students coming through the first funnel during the sorting process will differ depending on the demographics of a particular school. A higher percentage of students can be expected to screen positive in schools where many students are English language learners and qualify for free and reduced-price lunch (Kuo et al., 2009). A higher prevalence of distress would also be expected in communities that have experienced a recent traumatic event, such as a shooting, suicide, or natural disaster.

Personalizing the EHC: Lupe and Celia

Lupe and Celia are 11-year-old students who take part in the EHC. Both students fill out the MFQ and have the same score of 22, which is above the cutoff for distress. This means that Celia and Lupe will meet individually with an EHC counselor, Ms. Gardner.

To get an overall impression of Celia and Lupe's emotional health temperature, Ms. Gardner reviews their screening questionnaires before the Check-In. Although Lupe and Celia came up with the same score, they filled out their questionnaires very differently, reflecting the fact that their distress is unique and not fully described by the total score. The girls did not endorse all of the same items, and when they did, they gave them different ratings. For example, Lupe endorsed the item "I felt miserable or unhappy" as sometimes true. When Celia rated the same item as true most of the time, it was cause for greater concern. In addition, some MFQ items are more worrisome than others. The item "I felt lonely" is not as extreme as "I thought nobody really loved me." Celia marked, "I hated myself." Lupe did not, but marked "I felt grumpy or cross with my parents." Reporting feeling grumpy with parents is typical of middle school students, while a student hating herself is more of a red flag.

In the Check-In, Ms. Gardner uses a semistructured interview approach to gather more information about each girl's emotional health. This information helps to confirm the presence or absence of distress. When distress is confirmed, the interview probes the source of the distress and how it is interfering in the student's life. To assist in her evaluation, Ms. Gardner asks Lupe and Celia questions about their thoughts, behaviors, and feelings related to life inside and outside of school.

Ms. Gardner finds many similarities between Lupe and Celia. Both girls come from families who have recently emigrated from Mexico and are struggling financially. Celia and Lupe were happy in elementary school, and both girls are motivated to do well in middle school. With the help of supportive teachers, they have made gains in their acquisition of English. Now, as they transition to middle school, they are stressed by homework assignments and do not always understand what is expected of them. They are concerned about their appearance and worry that their clothes are not stylish. At this point in the EHC, Ms. Gardner has learned that both Celia and Lupe are true positives. They both show distress related to academic and social concerns. At this stage of the Check-In, Ms. Gardner will begin to sort out whether either girl needs a Support Plan.

Chapter 4

Evaluating the Need for a Support Plan

Evaluating Stressors

During the Student Check-In, the EHC counselor sorts out which students are in need of a Support Plan. This determination is made after gathering more information about the severity of the stressors and exploring the strength of the student's emotional health resources. If the severity of the stressors outweighs the strength of the resources, the counselor and the student develop a Support Plan.

Although many types of stressors affect middle school students, not all stressors are equal. Routine stressors, like being late for class, having a teacher whose instructions are difficult to understand, or walking into a noisy lunchroom to find a place to eat, are situations that many students encounter as they start the school year. Major stressors, like being teased in the lunchroom, struggling with a learning disability, or being sent to detention, are affecting a smaller subset of students. Severe stressors, such as food or housing insecurity, a death in the family, or a relative's deployment in the military, occur with less frequency. Some students have been exposed to traumatic stressors, like cruel treatment or witnessing violence.

Evaluating Strengths

After the severity of the stressors has been evaluated, the counselor explores the student's emotional health strengths. An assessment of strengths is used both to decide which students need bolstering and to identify resources that the student can build upon to formulate a Support Plan. The EHC organizes strengths into four categories:

1. Support network
2. Interpersonal skills
3. Coping strategies
4. Self-confidence

The Strengths Puzzle

Emotional health strengths can be viewed like the pieces of a puzzle. Once the EHC counselor learns about the shapes and sizes of the puzzle pieces, she can determine whether the student needs support. A student with missing or inadequately formed puzzle pieces will have a harder time managing stressors than a student with a complete puzzle.

SUPPORT NETWORK

One puzzle piece represents the student's support network. A support network is made up of family, friends, neighbors, teachers, and other community members. Having a network of supportive relationships contributes to emotional well-being by promoting a feeling of security, self-worth, and a general sense of belonging (Cohen, 2004). Strong support enables a student to face stressful experiences. Many students have a strong and effective cheering squad of family and friends to help them when life gets stressful. Some have

a professional helper on their team. When the student gets overwhelmed, someone is there to lend a hand. Other students have very weak networks, and some feel that they have no one to turn to.

Some students have support networks, but they are not activated. There are times when members of a network are distracted or unable to help due to the demands of their own circumstances. Caregivers who are ill, have a lot going on at work, or are overwhelmed by their own distress may find it difficult to devote time to the distressed student. Understanding the support network and how it functions helps the EHC counselor determine the need for a Support Plan and suggest people who could be called upon to be part of a plan.

INTERPERSONAL SKILLS

A second piece in the strengths puzzle symbolizes the student's interpersonal skills. These skills are used every day to interact with other people. Students with strong interpersonal skills are able to work productively in groups, communicate effectively, and resolve conflicts when they arise with peers and adults. These forms of social competence help students develop friendships, which in turn strengthen their social networks. In addition, students who experience fewer conflicts with teachers and are perceived as socially competent invite fewer disciplinary actions (O'Connell, Boat, & Warner, 2009).

COPING STRATEGIES

A third puzzle piece represents the coping strategies students use to deal with stressful situations. How a student sizes up challenges and manages thoughts, emotions, and behavior will be critical to middle school adjustment. Students who have a variety of positive coping strategies are able to address distress more successfully. Positive coping strategies include:

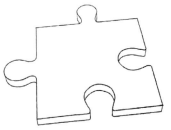

- *Problem solving:* The student identifies problems, generates solutions, and takes appropriate action.

- Information seeking: The student seeks out and uses information to solve problems.

- Self-regulation skills: The student uses deep breathing, counting to 10, or other self-management techniques to stay calm, focused, and alert. These strategies enable the student to think clearly about options and make thoughtful choices about how to behave.

- Help seeking: The student knows when he or she needs assistance, how to find help, and how to ask for it.

Students with fewer positive coping strategies are less able to manage stress and more likely to experience distress. Students who use positive strategies such as asking an older sibling for advice about managing a rocky friendship will be more likely to manage social stress than students who do not ask for help.

SELF-CONFIDENCE

The fourth puzzle piece symbolizes self-confidence. Self-confidence can influence a student's response to the stress of encountering new situations (Schunk, 1991; Druckman & Bjork, 1994). Self-confidence enables a middle school student to try out new coping strategies or to take steps to build a support network. Low confidence works in the opposite direction. Many factors contribute to low self-confidence, including harsh criticism, put-downs, flunking a quiz, or being excluded from the social mainstream—in other words, routine situations that often arise during the transition to middle school contribute to low self-confidence. Confidence can be built and strengthened. Helping students connect to support as simple as homework help to improve grades or an after-school club to establish connections with peers can boost self-confidence.

Assembling the Puzzle

During the Student Check-In, each puzzle piece or strength is evaluated. The EHC counselor notes when a piece is missing or is underdeveloped. When the puzzle pieces are viewed together, they depict either a student with adequate strengths to manage stressors or a student with insufficient strengths to manage distress.

Personalizing Stressors

Nate is a student who scored 19 on the MFQ, one point above the cutoff for distress. Nate lives with his parents and younger sister. He is an energetic kid who loves physical activity. Nate has a lot of friends, but most of them go to a different middle school, and he misses them. He is small for his age and is feeling frustrated that he has not been able to play in the lunchtime basketball games, because they are dominated by the older, bigger kids. He has been late to class several times because he finds it hard to change clothes after gym and get to the math classroom at the other end of the building. Nate's math teacher gave him a lunch detention last week for repeated tardiness.

Nate is stressed about his social life and worried that he will get another detention and be in trouble at home when his parents find out. The EHC counselor finds that Nate is disconnected from peers and in conflict with a teacher. His primary stressor is social.

Malik also scored high for distress on the MFQ. Malik is an only child who has always been an easygoing kid. He is a good student and has a large group of friends. However, since he started middle school, Malik has been having trouble concentrating. A few weeks before school started, his parents separated, and he is preoccupied with worries about the separation and what will happen to him if his parents get divorced. He is not turning in his homework assignments. In most classes he sits in the back and doesn't contribute to discussions. He is having trouble getting to sleep at night and is tired most days. He has been skipping football practice because he says it is not fun anymore.

Malik's parents are aware that he is upset, and a teacher called them recently to report that he is falling behind. His parents pushed a reluctant Malik to see a counselor to help him cope with their separation and potential divorce. The EHC counselor is concerned about Malik's social isolation and academic challenges. His primary stressor is emotional.

Personalizing Strengths

SUPPORT NETWORK

Nate has a support network that includes his parents and several aunts and uncles who live nearby. He has a large group of friends, but he is currently cut off from this part of his social network because his friends are attending a different middle school. His parents are not yet aware of the extent of his academic concerns, and Nate has not established a positive connection with any of his new middle school teachers. He has a support network that is not activated.

Malik's parents have arranged for him to see a counselor to talk about their marital separation. One of Malik's teachers has taken note of his poor concentration and slipping performance. The teacher has scheduled a meeting with his parents. Like Nate, Malik has a large group of friends, but is somewhat isolated since he stopped attending football practice. His parents, counselor, teacher, and football coach are aware of his depression and are actively working to ease his distress. Malik has a strong and activated support network.

INTERPERSONAL SKILLS

The counselor notes that throughout the interview Nate is soft spoken, hesitant, and rarely makes eye contact. Nate admits that he does not know how to figure out a good way to get into the basketball game at noon or to get to math on time. Nate's social skills could use strengthening.

Although Malik appears depressed, he looks the counselor directly in the eye and speaks clearly about the anger he feels about his parents' separation. With urging from his counselor, he is using his interpersonal skills to communicate with his parents and has decided to talk to the coach about what's been going on at home and about rejoining the football team. Although distressed, Malik is still using his strong interpersonal skills.

COPING STRATEGIES

Nate recognizes he is off to a bad start with his math teacher and wants to make a positive connection, but does not know how to make that happen. He has tried different ways to get into the noon basketball game, but all of his efforts have been unsuccessful. Nate

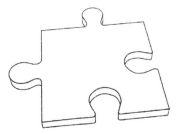

is stuck because he does not want his parents to know about his problems and also does not know whom else to ask for help. Nate is in need of new coping strategies.

The EHC counselor notices that Malik has made use of his support network and is beginning to take active steps to problem solve. Malik doesn't like feeling tired all day and has experimented with listening to music and reading to get to sleep at night. He agrees to work with a counselor even though he did not like the idea when his parents suggested it. Malik is using some coping strategies and may develop new ones in his upcoming counseling sessions.

SELF-CONFIDENCE

The EHC counselor assesses the level of self-confidence of both boys using observation and direct questioning. Both were asked to rate the question, "How confident do you feel that you can handle your problems?" On a scale of 1–10, Nate rates himself a 6. Malik rates himself a 5.

Nate seems to have a moderate level of self-confidence, but his confidence has faltered during the transition to middle school. Malik strikes the counselor as a confident adolescent who has lost his bearings due to the stress of his parents' separation.

Making the Support Plan Decision

In deciding whether to recommend a Support Plan, the EHC counselor carefully weighs each student's stressors and strengths. She does not recommend a Support Plan for Malik. Instead, she believes that with the extra supports he currently has in place, Malik will regain confidence and competence, things will get better, and he will get back on track. She commends him for his decision to accept help and work with a counselor while he is dealing with the stress of his parents' separation and the stressors related to starting middle school. She urges him to talk with his coach about rejoining the football team so he will not be so isolated from his friends. She encourages him to engage in other activities even when he might not feel like it and call on his support network if his distress remains high.

For Nate, the counselor recommends a Support Plan. She notes that his confidence has dropped since transitioning to middle school. The counselor commends Nate for his efforts to handle his problems, but notes that he needs support to make the positive changes he hopes for with teachers and peers.

Addressing Distress With a Student Support Plan

The EHC counselor and student develop a plan drawing on five strategies that address student distress:

1. Reduce stressors
2. Strengthen or activate the social support network
3. Improve interpersonal skills
4. Develop a variety of coping strategies
5. Build self-confidence

Working in collaboration with students and parents, the EHC counselor identifies strategies that will best address the emotional health needs of each student. The most common stressors affecting middle school students are academic and social challenges. During the Check-In, the counselor focuses questions on these areas while simultaneously observing and assessing the student's strengths.

Prior to Screening Day, the EHC team develops a list of school and community resources that serves as a menu of options during support planning. This list is based on a thorough inventory of the academic, social, and emotional health resources available at school and in the nearby community. The counselor uses the list to tailor individual plans without needing to reinvent a menu of options during each Student Check-In.

PERSONALIZING THE STUDENT SUPPORT PLAN

The EHC counselor and Nate work together to draft a plan to help reduce his distress, keeping in mind the five strategies. Nate agrees to meet with the school counselor to discuss getting to math on time and interacting more successfully with peers at lunch. He also agrees to talk with his parents about the detention and his desire to avoid future detentions and get along better with his math teacher. He says it is okay for the EHC counselor to talk with his parents about ways to get him reconnected to his old friends on weekends. She will discuss the connection to the school counselor with Nate's parents and reinforce the idea that the school counselor is a resource for parents, as well as students.

COMPLETING THE EHC: TYING IN WITH PARENTS

Following the Student Check-In, the EHC counselor engages the parent in a partnership during the Parent Phone Call. During this call, the EHC counselor shares feedback, solicits the parents' perspective, and enlists their help to put the Support Plan into action. Collaborating to determine what is needed will increase the chances of successful implementation of the Support Plan.

PERSONALIZING THE PARENT PHONE CALL

The EHC counselor calls the parents of Malik and Nate. The call to Malik's parents is brief. The counselor notes Malik's strengths and commends the efforts being made to support him. She lets Malik's parents know that she does not recommend additional support.

The call to Nate's parents is upbeat and starts with a review of Nate's strengths. The counselor then outlines Nate's stressors and an explanation of why she believes Nate is distressed. She works with Nate's parents to finalize and activate the Support Plan. Finally, she expresses confidence in Nate, his parents, and the plan.

Nate and Malik began their participation in the EHC with classroom screening and took part in individual meetings with the EHC counselor. Their involvement in the EHC concluded with a call to their parents. The Student Check-In yielded different outcomes for Nate and Malik, although they registered very similar emotional health temperatures. The EHC works systematically and efficiently to identify students who need to be linked to support. The EHC can be implemented at any middle school that decides it is a good fit for the needs of their students. A decision to move forward with the EHC should include a thoughtful process that involves all members of the school community.

Chapter 5

Getting the School on Board

The EHC Champion

The spark that ignites interest in the EHC may come from a variety of sources. Ideally, an individual or group of individuals will hear about the program and advocate for its implementation within their school community. One could think of this person or group as a champion. Champions might be school counselors, parents, the principal, a teacher, or community members committed to schools and improving student well-being. Two parents might read about the EHC and bring the idea to the principal. A school counselor might discuss the EHC with fellow special services staff and put it on a faculty meeting agenda. A champion might have a personal connection to a student who was overwhelmed by the transition to middle school. During the first phase of the EHC, the champion educates others and enlists the support of key members of the school community.

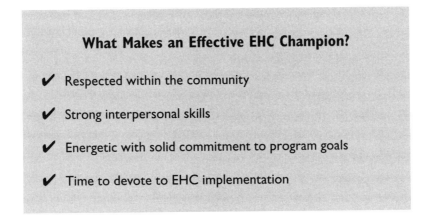

What Makes an Effective EHC Champion?

✔ Respected within the community

✔ Strong interpersonal skills

✔ Energetic with solid commitment to program goals

✔ Time to devote to EHC implementation

An effective champion knows that it takes more than a good idea to launch a new initiative. The champion discusses the EHC with key decision makers at the school or district level. Together they will consider a number of implementation factors. A decision to implement the EHC will include conversations about the school's openness to innovation. Decision makers will want to know how the program works, what outcomes they can expect, and what resources will be needed to both launch and sustain a program that addresses student emotional health needs. The champion should be prepared to discuss the following topics:

- The capacity of the school or district to implement the program with its available resources.

- Options for diverting or generating additional resources to support the leadership and workforce needed to implement and sustain the EHC program.

- How the EHC will fit a particular school setting and whether there will be a need to modify the basic EHC program.

- How the EHC will be introduced to members of the school community, including administrators, teachers, staff, and parents.

The Elevator Speech: Building a Team of Champions

As committed as any one champion might be to promoting emotional health in the school setting, implementing the EHC is not a one-person job. Individuals and groups will need to be convinced that the EHC is a good idea before a team can be engaged to make it happen.

The EHC champion composes a compelling message to generate enthusiasm and activate the school community. This message is a brief speech that contains a rationale and a summary of the EHC that could theoretically be delivered during a 1- to 2-minute elevator ride. An inspiring elevator speech provides listeners with a succinct overview of what is at stake for students and how the EHC benefits all members of the community. To get groups of stakeholders on board with implementing the EHC, the champion uses relevant language and examples tailored to the school. The elevator speech touches on these points:

- Stressors associated with the transition to middle school can cause emotional distress.

- Distress interferes with academic and social well-being.

- If unaddressed, distress can lead to serious problems like depression, anxiety, substance use, and school failure.

- Distress is difficult for teachers and parents to detect.

- The EHC detects and addresses student distress early in the transition to middle school.

- The EHC links distressed students to academic, social, and emotional health supports.

- The EHC is conducted at school to reach students who otherwise have poor access to health services.

- The EHC is designed to give every student an opportunity to be successful in middle school and beyond.

Using the elevator speech to share information about the EHC and its potential benefits can prove to be the spark that ignites interest within the broader school community.

Addressing Questions and Concerns

Implementing a new initiative in a school takes openness, resources, and commitment. The champion needs to be prepared to address concerns, questions, and possible misunderstandings. Not all members of a community share the same values, and the EHC may conflict with the beliefs of some constituents. Principals and administrators who have seen programs come and go over the years might be less than enthusiastic about the next new program, no matter how promising it sounds. Teachers worry about students who are struggling, but might have concerns about finding time and energy to embrace a new program that doesn't directly address academic achievement.

Some community members may believe that addressing student emotional health is not the responsibility of the school. The EHC takes place at school because school is the best place to reach the majority of young people. Studies have shown that between half and three quarters of children and adolescents who use mental health services are seen in schools and that, for many, school-based services are the only source of care (Farmer et al., 2003; Chatterji et al., 2004; Langer et al., 2015). Students from low-income households and students of color have disproportionately lower access to early identification and follow-up for mental health concerns unless they have access to school-based services (U.S. Public Health Service, 2000; Cassano & Fava, 2002; Garland et al., 2005; Mills et al., 2006; Weist, Rubin, Moore, Adelsheim, & Wrobel, 2007; Merikangas et al., 2011).

A concern may surface about whether sufficient resources are available to meet the needs of distressed students. The identification of distressed students will increase the demands on school resources. The EHC addresses this concern by taking a practical approach to identifying resources. When the EHC resource list is compiled, it includes formal and informal sources of support. Informal supports sometimes get overlooked but are capitalized on in the EHC. Getting students involved in after-school activities, setting up regular bedtimes or quiet study areas, or making a positive connection to the youth worker at church are examples of typical solutions written into Student Support Plans. The focus on activating family members, teachers, and school volunteers is in line with a prevention approach. Addressing stress before it causes distress and intervening early after distress surfaces means that most students can benefit from simple actions that will prevent smaller concerns from becoming larger problems.

For the EHC program to succeed, it is important to address questions such as these and to establish a climate of openness and trust. All stakeholders should have an opportunity to become acquainted with the program, have a chance to ask questions, and be informed about the potential costs and benefits of the EHC. Taking the time to meet face to face is the best way to educate community members and get them invested in the EHC program. Strategies include meeting individually with the principal or a small group of special services staff, communicating with faculty at their regularly scheduled faculty meetings, and writing articles for school bulletins. All community members want answers to the same questions:

What's in the EHC for students?

How will the EHC benefit our school?

And . . . what's in it for me?

Getting the Principal on Board

School principals are key stakeholders and decision makers. Therefore, it is critical to get the principal invested in the EHC early in the discussion. In some schools, the EHC champion will be a group of parents or a counselor who brings the idea to a principal who has no prior knowledge of the program. In this case, the champion will develop an elevator speech and engage in a discussion about the EHC with the principal. In other schools, the principal is the champion who works to get other members of the community informed and on board.

What's in It for Principals?

Principals and other administrators are concerned about the well-being and performance of their students and staff. Principals worry about student test scores and school progress reports. They know that their staff members are working hard, are carrying a heavy load of responsibilities, and are not fully equipped to address all student issues that surface. Principals have limited budgets and want to figure out the most cost-effective ways possible to support students. They understand that student distress increases burden on teachers and raises parent complaints.

Each day I hear from parents whose students are stressed. I wish we had better ways to ease their worries.—Mr. Alba

It's my responsibility to create a safe environment for all students. I need help from others to be the eyes and ears so that students do not fall through the cracks.—Ms. Geneva

The EHC offers support for the students and staff under the principal's supervision. It provides a structured, systematic approach to establishing positive connections between school, students, and parents. The EHC identifies and responds to a large number of students and presents an opportunity for a principal to provide extra training to faculty in the area of emotional health. Principals are reassured when every new student has had a checkup. In the end, the EHC helps to create safety, trust, and accountability within the school community. It addresses key impediments to academic achievement.

Ms. Garcia is the principal at a middle school with a faculty of 50 teachers and over 800 students. She wants all students to succeed. She works hard to support her staff, students, and parents. Attentive to the unique needs of the students transitioning to middle school, she has developed an orientation program for all incoming students and their parents. Before school starts in the fall, she leads parents on tours and outlines the changes and challenges ahead. However, with close to 300 incoming students, once school starts, she finds it difficult to know exactly who might be getting off track and falling behind.

Ms. Garcia attended all grade-level team meetings during the first week of school. She was happy to see that her first-year team was positive about the EHC. Her math teachers volunteered to give up a class period for Screening Day. When the EHC was over, several teachers expressed enthusiasm because more adults were getting involved with struggling students. Several commented that they had been contacted by parents to talk about how to bring up grades. Ms. Garcia is impressed that the program detected students who were struggling silently and is pleased that positive communication between her staff and parents is on the rise. To keep costs low, the EHC was implemented by her special services staff. She believes it has had a broad positive effect within her school community.

Ms. Garcia was the EHC champion at her middle school. Once she got her administrators and staff on board with the idea, she selected one of her school counselors to be the program coordinator, based on his ability to communicate and motivate. Her coordinator took the lead in educating the rest of the community, recruiting and training EHC team members, and creating broad support for the program.

Getting the Special Services Staff on Board

Most middle schools have one or more professionals on the staff who provide emotional health services. Representing disciplines such as school counseling, social work, psychology, and nursing, they provide a variety of special support services. These members of the helping professions have been trained to respond to the social, emotional, academic, and physical needs of a diverse student population. This group will want information about how the EHC works, its effectiveness, and how the program complements or adds value to the school's current emotional health services. The EHC leadership meets with these key stakeholders, scheduling enough time to discuss the aspects of the program that will be particularly relevant to them: the Student Check-In and specifically the development of the Support Plan.

What's in It for Special Services Staff?

The special services staff members worry that in the hustle and bustle at the start of the school year, some distressed students will be lost in the shuffle and fall behind. Most schools do not have adequate staffing to provide services to all students who need them. The daily schedules of many of these helping professionals are filled with responsibilities like academic scheduling, lunch duty, classroom presentations, and paperwork, all of which interfere with their ability to spend time getting to know students.

> At the start of the school year we quickly identify the kids who are having behavior difficulties, but we often miss the kids who are heading toward depression or anxiety and are suffering quietly.—nurse
>
> It's hard to fit it all in. . . . I do the course scheduling, make class changes, and assist in the orientation of all new students. If I had just one conference with each student, it would take me to the end of the school year.—counselor

The EHC assists the special services staff by screening all incoming students, confirming those who are distressed and narrowing down who is in need of help. The EHC counselors are allies who help to create positive connections and encourage students and parents to seek help. Special services staff appreciate that the EHC team increases their capacity to address student concerns, which helps them feel more successful in their goals to serve students. Student Support Plans developed by the EHC counselors often include connecting special services staff with distressed students they might otherwise miss.

Mr. Ino is the school counselor responsible for the youngest students at his urban middle school. In the first few months of school most of his time is spent changing schedules and dealing with behavior issues. He'd like to spend more time in direct contact with students and focus more on preventing problems than dealing with crises. Instead, his responsibilities and time constraints mean that he often relies on students to make requests to see him, operating in a come-and-get-it mode. With 250 students to sort through each fall, it's difficult to find and address the needs of the quieter kids.

Mr. Ino is the champion who spearheaded the EHC at his school. He worked with the principal and grade-level teachers to identify, orient, and motivate an EHC team. He enlisted his counseling interns and a few qualified community volunteers to help him conduct Student Check-Ins. He is grateful that the EHC uncovered the distress of quieter students at the start of the school year so that he was able to focus on their needs. He is pleased that many student problems were addressed early in the school year and is convinced that without the EHC, many of the students would have developed bigger problems.

Getting Teachers on Board

The champion approaches teachers in small groups to answer their questions and to allow adequate opportunity to foster a shared understanding and commitment. A meeting with the faculty who work with incoming students should include enough time to discuss the rationale and benefits of the EHC, as well as the logistics and impact of Screening Day and Check-In activities on instruction time. Teachers want information about role expectations and time commitments that will affect them in the performance of their academic responsibilities.

What's in It for Teachers?

Teachers worry about students who are struggling academically. They notice when a student is not turning in work or is falling asleep in the back row. They wonder about what is happening in student lives outside of school. Teachers are concerned about the impact that new grading standards and more rigorous homework assignments will have on incoming middle school students. Increasingly, they worry about the influence of social media on academic performance and of cyberbullying on emotional health. Teachers often feel that they do not have enough time, skill, or individual contact with students to identify or address emotional health problems.

> Just because mental health problems are not addressed at this middle school doesn't mean they do not exist. I wish I knew which of my quiet kids are having problems, especially my newcomers who don't speak English that well.—Ms. Singer
>
> I worry about the students who are socially immature and don't know how to handle pressure from the older kids. I think it really stresses some students a great deal.—Mr. Cooke
>
> Some kids are just plain distracted by peers and not organized enough. They start to fall behind almost immediately.—Mrs. King

Teachers appreciate the opportunity to learn more about the warning signs of distress and the impact of emotional health problems on academic success. They are relieved when EHC counselors encourage students and parents to seek help. They find that the EHC helps students come to school ready to learn. Partnering with the EHC team to promote positive change for students, teachers feel more hopeful about the ability of all students to succeed.

Mr. Reid teaches language arts. It's October, and he has a few students who look as overwhelmed as they did the first week of school. With 150 students on his schedule, he is swamped grading homework assignments. Most kids are getting their homework done and turned in on time, but today he is meeting with a grandmother and her grandson who has yet to complete one assignment. He would say that most of his students seem on top of their work and respond to classroom rules, but a few are really out of touch and disengaged.

Mr. Reid encouraged his students to participate in the EHC classroom screening, and most of them did. Many of his students had Student Check-Ins. He was happy when he was contacted by two parents requesting homework help and learned that they were acting because of a Support Plan developed during the EHC. One of his students is now on the roster to be assessed for special education services. The gym teacher told him that, because of a Support Plan, a struggling student is transferring out of P.E. and will be the nurse's teaching assistant. The gym teacher says she hopes the reassignment will boost the student's confidence and enable the nurse to keep a close eye on her emotional health. Mr. Reid is already seeing positive results in his students.

Making the Big Decision

A thoughtful review by members of the school community leads to a decision about whether the EHC is the right fit for a particular middle school. The final decision as to whether to implement the EHC is made by the principal and a group of key stakeholders. Efforts to develop a critical mass of enthusiasm among faculty and special services staff will pay off when it comes to program implementation. Once the decision has been made to adopt the EHC, it is time to form an EHC team, inform parents, and ultimately prepare to carry out the program using the protocols, instructions, scripts, and tools found in Part II of this handbook.

PART II

A-to-Z Guide
for Implementing an
Emotional Health Checkup

Fasten your seatbelt. With detailed scripts, instructions, and examples, Part II guides the reader step by step through EHC implementation procedures. In-depth information is presented on how to introduce the EHC to parents and students, obtain parent permission, implement Screening Day, conduct the Student Check-In, develop a Support Plan, and make Parent Phone Calls.

Scripts embedded in Part II were written for the dual purposes of training the team and implementing the EHC. Woven into the scripts are student stories and coaching notes. Organizational tools for Screening Day are included, as are templates for developing Support Plans and tracking communications during the Parent Phone Call. Printable versions of all scripts and forms are found in Appendices B and C.

A note to the reader about language in Part II: After drawing clear distinctions between stress and distress in Part I, there are many places in the Part II scripts where the words "stressed" or "stressed out" are used for the concept of distress. The reason for this switch is that "stressed" and "stressed out" are more frequently spoken and easily understood by youth and their family members. Drawing the distinction between stress and distress, while hopefully helpful to the reader, is unnecessary during the actual implementation of the EHC. The text continues to use the words "parent," "mother," or "father" to make reading and the navigation of scripts easier. This is not meant to discount or fail to recognize the many relatives or unrelated adults who are primary caregivers of middle school students.

Chapter 6

The School Decides to Implement the EHC

The Program Coordinator Comes on Board

The principal and a group of key stakeholders select a program coordinator to lead the EHC team and oversee program implementation. The champion may or may not become the program coordinator, but ideally the coordinator is a school employee or community member with time clearly designated to oversee the EHC from start to finish.

The effective coordinator has the personal qualities needed to mobilize, motivate, train, and supervise a team and the ability to communicate well with district officials, faculty, parents, and students. Ideally, he or she will have teaching or training experience, an understanding of children's emotional health, and strong organizational skills. The coordinator will provide leadership that sets the EHC in motion and keeps all of the parts running smoothly. The coordinator has a long to-do list and may work in partnership with a champion or handle the following tasks independently.

- Orient all school staff to the EHC.

- Work out EHC logistics with teachers.

- Recruit and train an EHC team.

- Catalog school and community resources.

- Provide ongoing supervision to the team.

- Monitor and troubleshoot implementation activities.

- Keep in touch with school administrators.

- Conduct a program review.

- Report back to stakeholders once the EHC is completed.

Orientation of School Staff

The principal and program coordinator jointly draft a timeline for program implementation. They take stock of what community members already know and what else they might need to learn about adolescent emotional health or the EHC prior to implementation. It is a good idea for all staff members who come into contact with parents and students to be prepared to answer questions about the EHC program. School staff who are knowledgeable about and supportive of the EHC will encourage student participation and contribute to program success.

Discussing EHC Logistics With Teachers

The coordinator meets with grade-level faculty and other relevant school staff to discuss logistics for implementing EHC activities: informing parents and students, organizing Screening Day, and scheduling Student Check-Ins. Teachers work hand in hand with the coordinator to address the critical logistical issue of selecting the classrooms that will host screening activities. Teachers who host Screening Day will give up instruction time.

There are two approaches to scheduling Screening Day to reach all incoming students. In the first approach, Model A, the faculty chooses a single academic subject, such as math, that all students have in their schedules. Screening is implemented on one day in every math class throughout the day. The second approach, Model B, is to complete screening during a single class period, such as fourth period. Following this format, all students are screened in every subject that is taught fourth period. Faculty need to decide which model works best for them. In Model A, the EHC team coordinates Screening Day with a few math teachers. In Model B, all grade-level teachers who teach during fourth period are involved.

Imagine again a hypothetical middle school with 250 incoming students. The program coordinator meets with the grade-level faculty, who decide to use Model A. In this model, screening will take place during math class. There are two math teachers who together teach a total of 10 math classes each day. Two EHC teams, with three members each, are needed to implement classroom screening in all of the math classes in a single day. If, on the other hand, the faculty decides to use Model B, 10 EHC teams are needed to reach all 250 students during the ten grade-level classes taught fourth period. A school with only 80 students might decide that three teams could screen every student during fourth period on one day. The coordinator and faculty take into account the number of students and available screeners to decide which approach to take.

CLASS PERIOD	PERIOD 1	PERIOD 2	PERIOD 3	PERIOD 4	PERIOD 5	PERIOD 6
SCREENING MODEL A	2 math classes 6 EHC team members	2 math classes 6 EHC team members	2 math classes 6 EHC team members	1 math class 3 EHC team members	2 math classes 6 EHC team members	1 math class 3 EHC team members
SCREENING MODEL B				10 grade-level classes 30 EHC team members		

The Program Coordinator Assembles the EHC Team

Schools that decide to implement the EHC need to consider how to form and sustain an effective team that draws on the talents and resources available in their particular community. Implementation may be supported by district, local, or federal funding. When the EHC was first developed, federal funding supported a team of university personnel to implement and test the EHC within public middle schools in Seattle, Washington. The program was then sustained by gifts from a local philanthropist.

The program coordinator recruits the EHC team of classroom screeners and EHC counselors. Classroom screeners are responsible for implementing Screening Day in classroom settings. EHC counselors meet one-on-one with students to conduct Student Check-Ins. Both roles might be filled from within the school, the outside community, or a combination of the two. When deciding whether to recruit staff from inside or outside the school system, decision makers will need to consider multiple factors. A school with staffing flexibility and internal resources may enlist existing personnel and reassign their responsibilities to enable them to serve on the EHC team for a period of time. The school with external funding from a federal grant, foundation, or private donor may choose to hire community members. The following are three models for recruiting an EHC team.

RECRUITMENT MODEL A

In this model, school employees are selected to serve on the EHC team, and some portion of their job responsibilities are reassigned during the time-limited EHC implementation period. Assembling a team of people who know school protocols, are acquainted with students, and understand how the school operates will reduce training time and costs. It may be possible to reassign duties of administrators, counselors, or other support services staff to serve on the EHC team without adding the cost of extra salary support. Collaboration between the EHC team and other school personnel will be more efficient when people know each other and how to get things accomplished within school settings.

On the downside, using internal school staff complicates the steps needed to protect confidentiality. It may require a change in school culture to ask staff to refrain from discussing the responses on a student's questionnaire or what transpires during a Check-In. Creating conditions where students and parents feel comfortable sharing personal information may be especially difficult in smaller communities where most people know each other and where parents are employed at the school. Training that covers confidentiality and fulfilling multiple roles is essential.

RECRUITMENT MODEL B

In this model, the team is assembled from outside the school. Working with a team external to the school means that maintaining confidentiality is less complicated. Students may feel more willing to share personal information with adults who do not interact with them in other roles on a regular basis. Parents may appreciate that the EHC counselor is not the person who assigns their child grades or serves as a disciplinarian. They might feel more trusting knowing that private family information is not being shared among school personnel.

Enlisting outside community members adds to the number of adults working to benefit students. It may bring new expertise or skills into the school to complement and extend those of the school staff. While it may be possible that a group of volunteers would be willing to contribute their expertise to the school as members of the EHC team, there are almost always additional costs associated with creating an external team. Finding, orienting, and maintaining an external team will take time and effort and may introduce scheduling problems. When team members are not school employees, there will be a need to develop protocols for how they will interface with school personnel and adhere to school policies.

RECRUITMENT MODEL C

Recruitment Model C combines staff from inside the school with volunteers or contracted workers from the outside community. More important than the source of the team members is the qualities they bring to the team.

Recruiting the Classroom Screening Team

The coordinator recruits screeners who have experience interacting with middle school students. Ideally, screeners demonstrate strong classroom management skills and are comfortable communicating and setting limits with adolescents. Screeners might include trained volunteers or school staff reassigned temporarily to work on the EHC team. Teachers from other grade levels might be assigned to a team to screen during their prep period on Screening Day. Communities with community colleges or universities might partner with education or psychology departments to recruit student volunteers to work under the program coordinator. The program coordinator decides how many screeners will be needed based on logistical decisions made with grade-level faculty.

Recruiting EHC Counselors

When assembling the team, recruiting EHC counselors may present the greatest challenge. The university-based EHC team in Seattle recruited community social workers with master's degrees to serve as EHC counselors. Over the years, school counselors and interns pursuing degrees in school counseling or social work were also trained to conduct Check-Ins. EHC counselors should have a counseling or child mental health background, a demonstrated ability to communicate with students and parents, and a willingness to adhere to a semistructured assessment approach. Experience in assessment, treatment planning, and referral are desirable.

Depending on the makeup of the community and the preferences of decision makers, the EHC counselors may be recruited from within the special services staff in the EHC school or other schools in the district or be partners from university or community settings. If district-wide EHC implementation is underway, one model to consider is to recruit school counselors, social workers, or psychologists from two or more schools to work on an EHC team that serves all participating middle schools in the district.

Students who screen positive for distress should have a Check-In within one to three weeks following Screening Day. Each Check-In takes 30–40 minutes, meaning that most can be completed in one class period. The coordinator creates a Check-In schedule, anticipating the need to accommodate a few extended interviews, student absences, and special school events, such as assemblies or field trips. One EHC counselor might be scheduled to meet with four to six students a day. Depending on the time availability of counselors, the number of students anticipated to screen positive, and the time frame for completion of the Check-Ins, the coordinator decides how many counselors to recruit. Counselors with limited clinical experience will need supervision from a senior staff person or team member. Two or more counselors can provide each other peer support.

General Training of the EHC Team

The coordinator oversees the general training for all members of the EHC team who must understand EHC goals and procedures and the roles different team members play. The team will learn about the importance of maintaining confidentiality and school protocols that need to be synchronized with the EHC, as well as how to respond to questions and special circumstances that may arise. Topics covered in the general EHC training as well as the school community orientation are shown below. Specialized training of classroom screeners and EHC counselors is covered in Chapters 8 and 9.

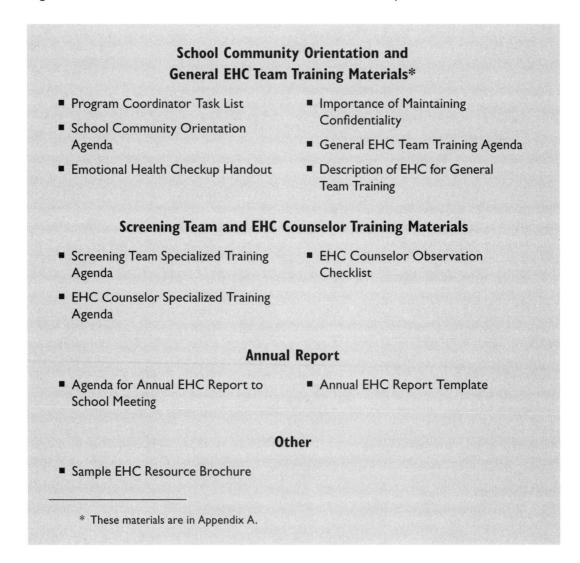

School Community Orientation and General EHC Team Training Materials*

- Program Coordinator Task List
- School Community Orientation Agenda
- Emotional Health Checkup Handout
- Importance of Maintaining Confidentiality
- General EHC Team Training Agenda
- Description of EHC for General Team Training

Screening Team and EHC Counselor Training Materials

- Screening Team Specialized Training Agenda
- EHC Counselor Specialized Training Agenda
- EHC Counselor Observation Checklist

Annual Report

- Agenda for Annual EHC Report to School Meeting
- Annual EHC Report Template

Other

- Sample EHC Resource Brochure

* These materials are in Appendix A.

Chapter 7

Engaging Parents and Students

What's in It for Parents?

Once the school is committed to implementing the EHC and the team is recruited, it is time to engage parents and students. Parents have many worries as their children approach middle school. They have heard rumors about students being bullied or getting lost in the shuffle. They wonder if their child is organized enough to keep up with homework demands. They may recall negative experiences they had in middle school and be concerned about what lies ahead for their child.

> Elsa and I are close, but I did not find out about her worries until after the EHC. I had no idea that every day she was stressed about how she looked and that it gave her a stomachache.—Kathryn

> Our son went to a small elementary school where the teachers were very aware and attentive. His middle school is really large. Unfortunately, he wasn't ready to deal with bullies. The EHC connected us with the school counselor, and it helped to know whom to call when we had a question or a concern.—Samuel

Parents benefit from the EHC in many ways. It is reassuring to parents that the school checks up with every student during the middle school transition. The EHC provides parents with general information about the nature of emotional health concerns common for middle school students and how to recognize the warning signs of adolescent emotional distress. Parents who do not get a phone call from an EHC counselor will know that their child did not report distress on Screening Day. Parents of students who do get a call receive either a reassuring message that their child is managing the transition well, or the message that there are resources to help get their child on track for success. Some parents will experience a positive connection with their child's school and will appreciate being introduced to adults who can support their child within the school setting. Over the years, parents have given positive feedback about the EHC (McCormick, Thompson, Vander Stoep, & McCauley, 2009).

When Helen's daughter, Kita, started middle school, she wasn't sharing much about school. Helen kept wondering if Kita was making friends and getting along okay. Helen hadn't heard from any teachers, so she assumed that Kita was keeping up with her work. She didn't have a clue that Kita was feeling burdened by all the homework. But she did seem moody. Other moms had warned Helen this might happen in middle school. When people asked, she realized that she wasn't really sure how Kita was doing.

Kita participated in the EHC classroom screening, showed signs of distress, and met privately with Suzan, an EHC counselor. Suzan called Helen and they talked about Kita's stress around homework and meeting her own high expectations. When Kita spoke with Suzan, she indicated a willingness to get academic help and wanted to devote more time to having fun, which was reassuring to Helen. Helen and Suzan confirmed a plan for Helen to set up a quiet homework area, monitor Kita's assignments, and connect her with the homework club. After speaking with Suzan, Helen started checking in regularly with Kita to find out more about what was going on at school.

Informing Parents

There are many ways to get the word out to parents (Vander Stoep et al., 2005). The EHC team brainstorms creative ideas for informing the parents in their community with a goal to reach all parents of incoming middle school students and ultimately to offer the EHC to as many students as possible. Not all parents will want their children to participate, but using jargon-free language to talk openly about emotional health and its role in academic success will improve the chances that families will opt to let their children take part. EHC team members make presentations at back-to-school nights and orientation events, write articles for school bulletins or newsletters, or use other school-specific mechanisms for communicating with parents.

By creating engaging parent educational materials, the EHC team aims to generate community-wide knowledge, interest, and enthusiasm. An investment in creative marketing sends the message that attending to student emotional health is a school priority. It also heightens awareness about the link between emotional health and school success and can reduce stigma related to emotional health issues. Bilingual staff are consulted about how to best communicate with non-English-speaking parents and describe the EHC using a culturally competent approach. Informational materials and permission forms are translated into the primary languages spoken by parents of students enrolled at the school. EHC information is sent home with each student a few weeks before Screening Day. A parent information packet includes the following:

- A letter from the principal encouraging families to participate

- A flyer with information about adolescent emotional health and an overview of Screening Day, the Student Check-In and Parent Phone Calls

- A parent permission form

Introducing the EHC to Students

A great deal of preparation is required before the screening team walks into a classroom and asks students to fill out a 30-item questionnaire. In the week or two prior to Screening Day, the EHC team gives students a short presentation, called the Student Introduction. During Student Introductions, team members explain how the transition to middle school can be stressful and why some students need support to get on track. They describe how the EHC connects distressed students with an adult who helps them sort out what they need to feel less stressed. New middle school students like knowing that they and their friends are being cared for. When made aware of how students might benefit from the EHC, they are more likely to ask their parents for permission to participate.

To avoid taking up too much instructional time, the team uses a script, an adaptation of the elevator speech for students. The program coordinator decides who will conduct the Student Introductions and uses the introduction script below.

Instructions in the script are in plain text and in brackets. What the team member says to students appears in italics.

The Student Introduction Script

Hi, I am from the Emotional Health Checkup team. I'm here to tell you about a program that we offer to all first-year middle school students in the fall. We want to learn how you are doing and how we can best support you. Today we are going to introduce you to the Emotional Health Checkup and then hand out permission forms for you to take home to your parent or guardian. We are inviting all students to participate.

We know that starting middle school means a lot of changes, and change can be stressful. You are all starting a new school; you now have five or six teachers every day; and you probably have more homework.

How many of you have more homework than you did in elementary school? **[Solicit responses to get the students interacting with the speaker.]**

As you get older, you will find that students need to get a physical before they turn out for sports to make sure they are ready to play. The Emotional Health Checkup is like a physical, except it is for emotional health. In the checkup you fill out a questionnaire that asks about how you are feeling and getting along in middle school so far. Students who show signs of stress will have a chance to meet with a counselor who can help get them connected to support. We want every student here to have a good start to middle school.

You are probably wondering how the checkup works. We'll come into classrooms one day next week to give the questionnaire to everyone with parent permission. The questionnaire takes about 10 to 15 minutes to fill out. It is a questionnaire, not a test. Does anyone know the difference between a questionnaire and a test? **[The team is looking for answers like "there are not right or wrong answers" and "you just want our opinions." If no student comes up with the answers, the team provides answers.]**

When you fill out the questionnaire, your answers will be confidential. Does anyone know what confidential means? **[Solicit answers from students and then say:]** *That's right. It means your answers are private. No one except our team will see your answers . . . not your teachers, not your classmates, not your parents.*

To get an Emotional Health Checkup, you have to have written parent permission. Today we will hand out information and permission forms for you to take home to your parent or guardian. Please take responsibility for showing the form to your parents, asking them to read and sign the permission form, and bringing the form back to class with a parent signature. Your parent or guardian can say "yes," meaning they want you to have a checkup, or "no," meaning they do not want you to have a checkup.

[Optional: We have found it is fun and rewarding to give students a small gift for bringing forms back to school with a parent signature. Small gifts like gel pens, suckers, or school supplies have been motivating. We have also used a raffle to generate excitement. Every student who returns a signed permission form is entered into a raffle that takes place on Screening Day. Raffle prizes have included items such as small stuffed animals, water bottles, or candy.]

[Optional: *We have a small gift to say thanks to each student who shows responsibility and returns a form with a parent signature.*

And/or: *We will enter every student who brings back a signed permission form into a raffle we will hold on Screening Day.***]**

Did everyone get a packet? Please raise your hand if you did not get a packet with a permission form. Does anyone have any questions?

Please take the packet home and show it to your parent. If you have a planner, write down a reminder to give the packet to your parent like it was a homework assignment, so that you won't forget. Make sure your parent fills out the permission slip and signs the form, and then you bring it back to this classroom.

We'll be back to collect the permission forms **[give out thank-you gifts, and enter your names in a raffle]***. Your teacher has an envelope for collecting forms. We hope you will take part in the Emotional Health Checkup. We want to help you and your friends get a good start to middle school. Thanks for your attention. And thanks to your teacher for helping out, too.*

The teacher collects permission forms for the team. A team member returns on several days to pick up forms and hand out thank-you gifts. This maintains the visibility of the program and reminds students who have not yet returned their forms. Either the teacher or a member of the team can hand out new forms to students who were absent or lost their forms.

Chapter 8

Classroom Screening Day

The Screening Team

On Screening Day, a three-person team, composed of a leader, an organizer, and a roamer, administers the MFQ. The leader is in charge of the classroom. She uses a script to ensure that all relevant points are covered and that the MFQ is administered systematically in every classroom. An organizer tracks permission forms, ensures that questionnaires get to the right students, and confirms that all completed questionnaires are collected. The roamer hands out pencils and packets and supports the leader and organizer by answering questions and assisting students who need individual help.

Specialized Training for the Screening Team

The screening team undergoes specialized training in how to perform the three roles. Their mission is to gather candid responses to personal questions from each participating student. By the end of Screening Day the team will have sorted students who are distressed from those who are not. To carry out their mission, the team is trained to follow the Screening Day script and protocols. When the MFQ is administered in a systematic way, the screening score will more accurately reflect a student's level of distress.

All team members are trained in the three screener roles to allow for staffing flexibility and ensure strong leadership in every classroom on Screening Day. Rehearsing scripts during training pays off in greater team confidence and competence in the classroom. Team members learn how to address frequently asked questions and how to help students who don't understand vocabulary words on the MFQ. The team is trained to assist individual students or classrooms of students with special needs. Additional training is provided to teams who lack experience with classroom management or interacting with middle school students. These teams will be given information and will practice skills for effective communication with adolescents and positive classroom management.

Staying Organized

Organization is the backbone of successful EHC implementation. The screening team uses a student roster for each classroom to keep track of which students have received a parent packet and have parent permission to participate on Screening Day (see the example below). The same rosters can be used to document completion of the MFQ. It is important to maintain organized lists so that only students with parent permission fill out the questionnaire. When Screening Day is over, and the questionnaires are scored, the rosters can be used to organize the Student Check-Ins.

Student Roster			
Screening Class: Mr. Smith Period 1 Room 302 Screening Day: 10/16			
STUDENT NAME	PARENT PERMISSION STATUS	SCREENING DAY MFQ STATUS	NOTES
Lucy Adams	Yes	Completed	
Doug Sanchez	No		Did not return form
Sam Tang	Yes	Absent	Schedule makeup

Creating a Classroom Atmosphere Conducive to Screening

Maintaining a quiet and calm atmosphere during screening enables students to give thoughtful responses to the MFQ questions. This requires the team to interact with students in a friendly but firm manner. Screening team members learn how to convey behavior guidelines clearly. They ask that students raise a hand to ask a question, work quietly until all students have finished their questionnaires, and not talk with other students. The screening team uses positive behavior management strategies to maintain an orderly classroom environment. For example, the team praises students who listen and stay on task. While students are filling out their questionnaires, the team circulates within the classroom. They intervene with students who are not following directions, are talking to others, or are being disruptive.

Students can be distracted by the idea that some students are participating and some are not. The team minimizes distraction by giving each student a screening packet. Packets for students with parent permission contain the cover sheet, a screening questionnaire, and a fun activity like a word puzzle to keep students busy after they complete the questionnaire. Packets for students without parent permission include only the cover sheet and the fun activity. Screening Day classroom management tips are found in Appendix B.

Maintaining Confidentiality

The screening team learns about the importance of maintaining confidentiality during general EHC training. During their specialized training, they learn the specific techniques described below to maintain confidentiality in the classroom setting. The organizer labels each packet in a way to ensure confidentiality (Vander Stoep et al., 2005). The MFQ is labeled with an ID number, not the student's name. The name appears on a cover sheet that will be removed after screening. Only ID numbers remain on the completed questionnaires. The organizer keeps a secure list that has names matched to ID numbers, ensuring that no one except the EHC team knows which answers came from which student.

The team takes steps to maximize privacy in the classroom space. In middle school students often sit at tables, not individual desks. To promote privacy, the team directs students to rearrange seating, set up barriers with books, notebooks, or backpacks and use paper to cover their answers. Some schools have invested in commercially available cardboard barriers that students use for test taking. These can be put to good use on Screening Day.

The teacher is asked to remain at his desk while students are filling out their questionnaires. This gives students reassurance that the teacher will not look at their answers. However, since teachers know students best, their assistance is helpful with organizational activities like taking attendance and making sure that each student gets the correct screening packet. The teacher can also support the screening team with positive classroom management.

Screening Day Is Here

On Screening Day, the screening team comes to the classroom with the student roster, the screening script, and the screening packets. The team is set to administer the MFQ using a standardized script so that instructions are conveyed clearly, completely, and uniformly. The screening script guides the team through Screening Day. Instructions in the script are in plain text and brackets. What the team member says to students appears in italics. Training tips are in plain text without brackets.

Within a single 45–50-minute class period, the screening team completes four activities:

1. Introduce the EHC and collect permission forms (10 minutes)
2. Give general instructions (10 minutes)
3. Administer the questionnaire (20 minutes)
4. Wrap up Screening Day (5 minutes)

First Activity: Introduce the EHC

The leader introduces the EHC team members, takes attendance, and tells students about the purpose of the EHC.

Hi, I'm [name], *and this is* [introduce organizer and roamer]. *We are on the Emotional Health Checkup team. All of you have just started middle school. As you know, there are a lot of changes that students go through at this time. Change can be stressful. Everyone gets stressed sometimes. But being really stressed for a long time can be hard. It can lead to feeling unhappy, getting behind in schoolwork, and can take the fun out of being with friends. The Emotional Health Checkup is here to help you and your classmates feel less stressed. We want to make sure to give students the support they need so that each of you will have a good start to middle school.*

When we came to your class before we talked about how students need to get a physical checkup before they turn out for sports. It is also important for students to get an emotional health checkup as they face the challenges of starting middle school. The first step of the checkup is filling out a questionnaire. That is what we are doing today.

[Collect any permission forms students have brought to class.]

Before we begin, does anyone have a permission slip to turn in? If you do, please raise your hand.

The roamer picks up any new permission forms. The organizer prepares screening packets for students who have just brought their forms from home and updates the student roster.

Second Activity: Give General Instructions

The leader describes the screening process, what it means to fill out the questionnaire, and what will happen if a student is showing signs of distress.

We are inviting all students in your grade to fill out the emotional health questionnaire. The questionnaire takes about 10–15 minutes to complete. After we collect the questionnaires, we look at them. If your answers show us that you might be feeling stressed, a counselor from our team will check in with you in the next week to talk with you more about how you are doing. At that time, if you need help, we'll work together to make a plan so you can feel less stressed.

Here are some other things we want you to know about the questionnaire: We ask everyone the same questions. Also, your answers are confidential. Can anyone remember what confidential means?

[Call on students to answer the question to get them involved and keep them listening. Repeat and expand on student responses so that everyone hears the correct answer to the question. Thank students for contributing, or provide answers if no students volunteer.]

Thanks! That's right. It means that the answers you give on the questionnaire are private, and we won't share them with anyone: not your parents or your teachers or anyone else. Take a look and you will notice that there is an ID number, not your name, on the top of the questionnaire **[show]**. *That number is not your school ID number; it's a number we made up for each student just for the Emotional Health Checkup. The reason we use ID numbers is so that when you are finished, we can take the cover sheet off the questionnaire packet. That way your name is not on the questionnaire with your answers. No one except us will know it is your questionnaire.*

You are filling out a questionnaire, not taking a test. Can anyone tell the class about the difference between a questionnaire and a test?

[Call on students to answer, or provide answers if no students volunteer.]

Thanks! Yes, you won't be graded, and the questionnaire has no right or wrong answers. We want you to give answers that are true for you.

Some of the questions may be confusing. If you don't understand something, please raise your hand, and we'll come help you. Does anyone have a question right now? **[Pause to answer questions from students.]** *Okay, we are ready to hand out the packets.*

[Now is the time to address privacy. The leader tells students how to arrange for privacy and asks students who are not completing the questionnaire for their cooperation.]

At this point, let's take a moment for you to make a private space for yourself so others won't see your answers.

[Here are some options for the leader to say:

- *Since there are some extra desks, let's have you spread out to create more space for everyone.*

- *I understand your class has privacy screens, so please put one up just like you do when you are taking a test.*

- *Take out a sheet of paper, and you can use it to cover up answers while completing the questionnaire.*

- *You can use your notebooks or textbooks to make a small barrier between you and your neighbors to create a private space.*

The organizer and roamer hand out screening packets.]

If you want to participate and don't have a permission form, you can still bring one in later and turn it in at the office. Next week we'll be giving questionnaires to students who are absent today or who bring in their permission forms later.

Everybody will get a packet today. Please keep your packet on your desk until I say to open it. There are two different kinds of packets. Students who do not have parent permission have a packet with a word puzzle but no questionnaire. We would like you to work quietly on your word puzzle, read, or do homework so that students who are filling out the questionnaire can give thoughtful answers. Does that make sense to everybody?

Third Activity: Administer the Questionnaire

The leader now tells students how to fill out the MFQ. She uses a questionnaire as a prop.

For students who have parent permission and are completing the screening questionnaire, I want to show you how to fill it out before you begin. Please don't start until we've gone through all the directions. It's really important to answer these questions honestly, so please read the questions carefully, take time to think, and then answer truthfully. If you need help reading or understanding something, just raise your hand, and we will come help you. You can take as much time as you need.

If you have a questionnaire, please open it now and find the page that says Mood and Feelings Questionnaire at the top. Let's read the instructions together: "This form is about how you might have been feeling or acting lately. For each question, please mark how much you have felt or acted this way in the past two weeks." This means that we are not asking how you are feeling today and not how you have felt your whole life, but how you have been feeling over the past two weeks. That means the time from **[date 2 weeks ago]** *until today. Is that clear?*

Again, this is not a test, and there are no right or wrong answers. Please just make an X in the box for the answer that best describes you. Think about what your life at school, at home, and with your friends has been like in the past two weeks. Remember, you are the expert.

- *If a sentence was true about you most of the time during the past two weeks, mark an X in the box for "true."*

- *If a sentence was only sometimes true, mark an X in the box for "sometimes."*

- *If a sentence was not true about you in the past two weeks, mark an X in the box for "not true."*

Let's look at the first question together. Sentence number one says, "I felt miserable or unhappy." Think about yourself over the past two weeks. If you were feeling miserable or unhappy most of the time from **[date 2 weeks ago]** *to today, mark "true." If you were feeling miserable or unhappy some of the time, mark "sometimes." If you were not feeling miserable or unhappy in the past two weeks, mark "not true." Mark an X in the box for the answer that is closest to how you felt. Does anyone have a question?*

If you don't want to answer a particular question, you can choose to skip it. But don't skip a question just because you don't understand it. Any time you don't understand something, raise your hand, and we can help you figure it out. Also raise your hand when you are finished. We will come by and pick up your packet, and you can work quietly until everyone is finished. You can read a book, do homework, or work on the word puzzle.

You can start now. Go ahead and read and answer all of the questions one by one to the end.

The leader and roamer walk around the classroom to maintain a quiet atmosphere and make sure students are on task. They answer questions and praise students for their attention to completing the questionnaire or for working quietly at their desks. They intervene in the following situations:

- A student has a hand raised.

- A student is asking another student a question.

- A student has not turned in the questionnaire but is working on another activity.

- A student is noisy or leaves her desk without permission.

- A student is rushing or does not appear to be reading the questionnaire.

- A student looks confused or upset.

The leader and roamer pick up completed questionnaires and check for missed responses. When a student has completed the MFQ and is raising his hand, they attend to the student and say:

Thanks. I want to quickly check over your questionnaire to make sure you didn't miss any items that you didn't want to skip.

A screener scans quickly over all the items. If an item is blank, the screener asks the student quietly:

Did you mean to skip this one, or did you just miss it? It's really easy to miss a question.

Most students want the chance to answer a missed question. However, it is not a problem if a student skips an item intentionally; students have the right to opt out of answering any question. Completed questionnaires are handed to the organizer, who updates the student roster and keeps track of forms. Once all questionnaires are accounted for, the leader again addresses the class.

Fourth Activity: Wrap Up Screening Day

Thanking students is a way to end Screening Day on an upbeat note. Filling out a questionnaire that asks personal questions takes energy and may in itself be stressful. Working quietly so that other students can complete the questionnaire in a thoughtful way is courteous. The end of the class period is a good time to thank all students, whether or not they participated in screening.

It looks like everyone is done. I want to thank you all for working quietly while students filled out the questionnaires. And thank you students who filled out the questionnaires. I know it took energy and I appreciate your thoughtfulness. And thank you [teacher name] *for hosting us today. We appreciate that you gave up a day of math for the Emotional Health Checkup.*

[Optional: A verbal thank-you can be accompanied by a small reward, like a sticker, a snack, or a pencil. This would also be the time for a raffle, if one has been promised as part of the EHC.]

Maintaining a positive attitude on Screening Day from start to finish underscores the message that emotional health is a topic that can be discussed at school. It also communicates that the EHC is being carried out to help all students through a transition that can be stressful.

Scoring Screening Questionnaires

Over the course of Screening Day, EHC team members may have time to begin scoring questionnaires. The team scores the MFQ by adding up the points for each item, giving no points for "not true," one point for "sometimes true," and two points for "true most of the time." The minimum possible MFQ score is zero, and the maximum possible score is 60. A list is generated of students with scores of 18 or above, the EHC cutoff score indicating that students are showing signs of distress. This list is then handed over to the EHC counselors, who will schedule Student Check-Ins.

Occasionally, scoring anomalies surface that warrant special consideration. If a student does not answer every question, it is hard to interpret the total score. The team uses its judgment to decide how to proceed. When MFQ scores are hard to interpret—for example, a student has a score of 15 but has only completed half of the MFQ items—a team member can ask the student for clarification or go ahead and schedule a Check-In. If a student has completed 20 of the 30 questions, and the responses tally up to a total score of 3, then the team might either decide to classify the student as having screened negative or ask the student for clarification on the 10 missing items.

Handling Circumstances That Arise in the Classroom

Not everything on Screening Day goes according to the script. The screening team is trained to address a number of routine and exceptional situations that can arise in the classroom.

WHAT IF A STUDENT DOES NOT WANT TO PARTICIPATE IN SCREENING?

Some students do not want to participate in the EHC, even though a parent has given permission for them to do so. If this is the case, the organizer removes the questionnaire from the packet and gives the student a word puzzle with instructions to work quietly. The response to students who choose not to complete the screening questionnaire contains three messages:

1. The EHC team is comfortable with the decision.
     Yes, you can decide not to complete the questionnaire. The checkup is voluntary, so you get to

decide. However, your parent did give permission, so we'll need to remind them that the EHC is volun-tary and let them know that you decided to opt out.

2. **The team appreciates the student's thoughtful consideration of participation.**

   Thank you for considering being part of the checkup. You can work quietly on the word puzzle, read, or do homework.

3. **The team leaves the door open in case the student decides to participate.**

   If you change your mind, let me know, and I will give you your questionnaire, or you can fill it out on a later date.

WHAT IF A STUDENT DOESN'T UNDERSTAND SOMETHING ON THE QUESTIONNAIRE?

Students sometimes skip a question, not because they do not want to answer it, but because they do not understand it. Hearing a screener read the question aloud will usually settle confusion about words or phrases. Sometimes a student will want help choosing an answer. In this case, the screener holds back from giving help in decision making. Instead, she can read the question and options out loud and then encourage the student to choose the answer that most closely aligns with his or her experience.

Use one or more of these common strategies for responding to students who don't understand something on the questionnaire:

- Read the question aloud slowly.

- Ask if a particular part of the question is confusing, and then clarify.

- Use an EHC glossary to define frequently misunderstood words.

- Encourage the student to choose the answer that is best for him or her—the one that is "most true for you."

- Praise students for taking time to think through questions that are difficult for them.

WHAT IF A STUDENT COMPLAINS ABOUT THE QUESTIONNAIRE?

A student might complain that the questionnaire is too long or too confusing, or that the questions are stupid. Screeners should remain positive, not join in the criticism of the questionnaire or the EHC, and use these common strategies for dealing with complaints:

- Empathize with the student's difficulties.

   I'm sorry this has been confusing or difficult.

■ Offer the student options to make the experience easier. For example, offer to read items aloud; go more slowly; clarify any items they don't understand.

Thanks for hanging in there. This part can be tough. Let me see if I can help. I'll read the question out loud and see if that helps. Your responses let us know whether or not you are stressed and need help with anything.

WHAT IF A STUDENT WANTS TO PARTICIPATE ON SCREENING DAY BUT DOES NOT HAVE A SIGNED PERMISSION FORM?

The screening team schedules make up opportunities for students who are absent or bring permission forms to school after Screening Day. Makeup screening can be done during homeroom periods or lunchtime to minimize the loss of instruction time. Individuals or small groups of students meet with a screener in the school library or other designated location to go through the directions and complete the questionnaire.

WHAT IF A STUDENT BECOMES STRESSED WHILE COMPLETING THE MFQ?

On rare occasions, a student might become uncomfortable while completing the questionnaire. Members of the screening team will look for signs of discomfort such as a student who lays his head on the desk or appears restless and fidgety. A screener can quietly ask how the student is doing and encourage him to take a break, take a few deep breaths, or skip a question. Students can be offered the option of completing the questionnaire on a makeup day.

WHAT ABOUT ACCOMMODATING STUDENTS WITH SPECIAL NEEDS?

The EHC is designed to extend the reach of emotional health screening to as many students as possible. The MFQ can be completed by students who have a third-grade reading level, but the team may need to give extra assistance to whole classrooms or to individual students. A modified screening protocol can be implemented with English language learners or with students who have learning disabilities or behavioral or physical challenges. Modifications might consist of reviewing the vocabulary words and the meaning of the response options with a class in advance of Screening Day. Arrangements can be made for screeners to read all questions aloud with individual students or with an entire classroom. If English comprehension challenges are anticipated for a large number of students, the program coordinator can recruit bilingual staff to serve on the screening team. An instructional assistant can be asked to work one on one with a student to translate the questionnaire into American Sign Language. Whenever the screening team is unable to address the needs of individual students on Screening Day, arrangements can be made for students to complete the MFQ on a makeup day with a personal screener and, if needed, with assistance from a bilingual or special education staff person.

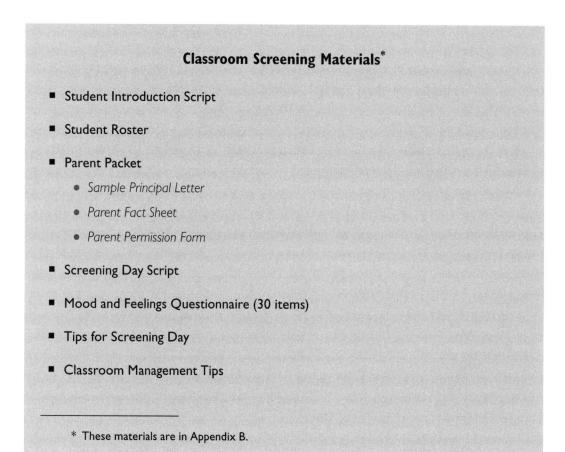

Classroom Screening Materials*

- Student Introduction Script

- Student Roster

- Parent Packet
  - *Sample Principal Letter*
  - *Parent Fact Sheet*
  - *Parent Permission Form*

- Screening Day Script

- Mood and Feelings Questionnaire (30 items)

- Tips for Screening Day

- Classroom Management Tips

---

* These materials are in Appendix B.

Chapter 9

The Student Check-In

Introducing the Check-In

Student Check-Ins are scheduled as soon as possible after Screening Day. The Check-In is structured to provide an opportunity for students to engage with an EHC counselor to identify areas of concern, areas of strength, and practical solutions for reducing distress. Establishing good rapport and a spirit of collaboration contributes to the success of the Check-In. The goals of the Student Check-In are to:

- Confirm whether or not the student is distressed. This is determined through a review of the MFQ.

- Understand the degree to which distress is interfering with the student's overall functioning. This involves an assessment of how well the student is doing academically, socially, and emotionally.

- Determine which students need a Support Plan. The counselor evaluates a student's level of distress in relation to his or her personal strengths and support network.

- Partner with the student to develop a straightforward action plan to provide academic, social, or emotional health support, as needed.

The Student Check-In is designed to lead to one of three dispositions, or conclusions, about the student's emotional health status:

1. The student is not truly distressed.
   No Support Plan is needed.
2. The student is distressed but has the necessary skills, confidence, and support to manage distress.
   No Support Plan is needed.
3. The student is distressed and lacks the necessary skills, confidence, and support to relieve distress.
   A Support Plan is needed.

Specialized Training for EHC Counselors

The EHC counselors undergo specialized training in how to conduct the Student Check-In and Parent Phone Call. The role of the EHC counselor is different from that of a mental health counselor, who provides treatment. The role of the EHC counselor is to assess three potential sources of distress: academic, social, and emotional. Counselors are trained to carry out a one-time structured assessment, using their clinical judgment to evaluate a wide range of problems. The EHC approach promotes interactions that recognize students and parents as experts and partners, identify and build on strengths, encourage help seeking, and instill hope that things can get better.

Several general principles guide training. The focus on three areas of functioning—academic, social, and emotional—is different from academic counseling or mental health counseling, which generally target a single area. A strength-based approach emphasizes the student's personal strengths and resourcefulness. A partnership model encourages students and parents to engage as full partners in all aspects of the planning and linkage to support. Support plans link students to informal as well as formal resources.

Counselors use a combination of ratings and conversation within a problem-solving framework to efficiently gather a great deal of information in a short period of time. Problems are identified, solutions generated and evaluated, barriers addressed, and finally a Support Plan is drafted with the student to share with the parent. Counselors synthesize information quickly and draw on the EHC resource list to make recommendations for the Support Plan.

Check-In training is a graduated process that includes a combination of didactics, modeling, and active practice in which EHC counselors:

1. Review the principles that guide the Check-In.
2. Are oriented to the materials and instructions and read through all scripts aloud as a group.
3. Observe a role-play conducted by the program coordinator, a supervisor, or an experienced EHC counselor.
4. Practice components of the Check-In through role-play.
5. Conduct a supervised Check-In and Parent Phone Call.

How to Conduct the Student Check-In

The Check-Ins are conducted in a private meeting space at school. EHC counselors have a list of students who screened positive. For each Check-In, a counselor needs to have the student's MFQ questionnaire, a Check-In script, a Decision Grid, and a Support Plan template.

The Check-In includes four activities:

1. Introduce the Check-In (5 minutes).
2. Assess stressors and key areas of strength (15 minutes).
3. Summarize impressions (5 minutes).
4. Develop a Support Plan (20 minutes).

Inviting Students to the Check-In

Students were told on Screening Day that they might be invited to meet with an EHC counselor if they showed signs of stress. Because help seeking for emotional health problems is often stigmatized, precautions are taken to protect the student's privacy and reduce the possibility of discomfort or labeling. The student is called from class to meet with the EHC counselor using the same procedures that are used to excuse a student for other reasons, such as a dentist appointment.

First Activity: Introduce the Check-In

Building a trusting alliance between the counselor and the student lays a foundation to meet the goals of the Student Check-In. The introduction to the Check-In should be upbeat and friendly. Because students who are called from class to meet with an adult often think that they are in trouble, they are told right up front that this is not a disciplinary meeting. During the introduction, the student learns about the goals for the Check-In, the role of the counselor, and the boundaries of confidentiality. The tone set at this stage will provide a foundation for a positive experience for the student.

The process of building trust begins the moment the EHC counselor first meets the student. Using good communication basics, the counselor greets the student warmly, makes direct eye contact, smiles, and offers a hand in greeting. The counselor shows interest and avoids using jargon or language that might confuse a middle school student.

Embedded in the introduction are several important elements:

- The counselor conveys enthusiasm about getting to know the student and working together, starting off with a statement such as: *Thanks for being willing to meet with me. I'm really happy to meet you and I am looking forward to hearing more about how things are going for you.*

- The counselor normalizes student distress by acknowledging that stress is a normal part of the transition to middle school, making comments such as: *Lots of kids are stressed out at the start of middle school.*

- The counselor conveys a sense of hope by communicating that change is possible, help is available, and things can get better: *I've worked with a lot of middle school students who were stressed out at the beginning of the year, and I know that with support, things can get better.*

The Check-In script that follows includes notes for training purposes. Training notes appear on the right side. What the counselor says to students appears in italics on the left with instructions in plain text. Suggestions for optional clarifying questions and prompts are also in italics, but appear in [brackets]. A printable version of the script without training notes is found in Appendix C.

CHECK-IN SCRIPT: INTRODUCTION	NOTES FOR THE EHC COUNSELOR
Hi. My name is **[name]**, *and I am part of the Emotional Health Checkup team. First of all, I want you to know you are not in trouble! I called you from class today to talk about how things are going for you here at middle school. Remember the questionnaire you filled out the other day in class? The questionnaire gives our team an idea of who might be feeling stressed. In the next few weeks I'll be meeting with lots of students to check on how things are going for them.*	**INTRODUCE THE CHECK-IN** ✔ Dispel concern that student might be in trouble. ✔ Normalize the meeting by telling students they are not the only student participating in the Check-In.
Thanks for taking the time to complete the questionnaire in class. Your questionnaire showed that you have been feeling stressed. I'm really glad to meet you so that I can hear more about how middle school is going and to see if there is anything we can do to support you so you can feel less stressed.	**INTRODUCE THE GOALS** ✔ Note the connection between the MFQ and the Check-In. ✔ Help the student relax, and note Check-In benefits.
I've worked with a lot of students who were stressed at the beginning of middle school, and I know there are ways to get support and feel better. I'll need your help because you are the expert on how middle school is going for you. 　*We can work together to make a plan in any areas where you may need or want some help. Sound okay?*	**INTRODUCE THE PARTNERSHIP** ✔ Assure students that they are active participants. ✔ Instill hope that things can get better if you work together.

CHECK-IN SCRIPT: INTRODUCTION (continued)	NOTES FOR THE EHC COUNSELOR
Before we go further, I want to talk with you about confidentiality. Your answers on the questionnaire were confidential or private, and only people on the EHC team could see the answers you gave. I want you to know that what we talk about today will also be confidential, and I will not share what you tell me with others, not your teachers, the principal, not even your parents, unless we agree on what to share. However, there are two exceptions to this. *First, I want you to know that if you tell me that you are going to hurt yourself or that someone is hurting you, I will share that information so we can make a plan to keep everyone safe. I will not do anything without talking with you first.* *And, second, after I meet with students, I call a parent to say thank you for letting them take part in the Emotional Health Checkup. I will call your parents to let them know that you missed a class to meet with me today. You and I will decide together if there is anything else I should talk to your parent about and what I will say. Do you have any questions about confidentiality or what I will share with others?*	INTRODUCE CONFIDENTIALITY ✔ Reassure students that most personal information will not be shared with others without their permission. ✔ Explain that to ensure safety, there are exceptions to confidentiality. ✔ Explain clearly what information might be shared with others. Students will be more comfortable once they know the rules of confidentiality. ✔ Inform students that a call to a parent is part of EHC protocol. ✔ Let students know that they help shape the call home.

Second Activity: Evaluate Stresses and Strengths

During the introduction to the Check-In, the counselor refers to the student's questionnaire and notes that it showed signs of distress. In general, the counselor treats the MFQ as a resource and does not review every item with the student. The counselor uses the interview to gather information about middle school in general, eliciting both facts and perceptions from the student that will be synthesized into an assessment of how the student is functioning.

Warm-up questions are used at the start of the assessment to help put the student at ease and to get an overview of the student's situation. They are intended to be easy to answer and nonthreatening, and to provide an orientation to the format of the interview. Ask the primary warm-up questions. Optional clarifying questions are provided in brackets.

CHECK-IN SCRIPT: WARM-UP QUESTIONS	NOTES FOR THE EHC COUNSELOR
To get started, I'd like to ask you a few questions about yourself. *Whom do you live with?* *How long have you lived in your current place?* *How many times have you moved since first grade?* Optional: [*How old are your siblings?* *Do they go to school here too?* *How much time do you spend with your family? How much time do you spend at Dad's house?* *When did you move here?* *When did your family move from Mexico?*] *What do you like to do for fun?* *Do you have any regular organized activities, like sports teams, band, scouts, or clubs?* Optional: [*Are you on a basketball team?* *What kind of music do you like to play?* *How much time do you spend practicing?* *Do you attend any of the after-school activities here at school?* *Are there activities you might like to try now that you are in middle school?*]	✔ Convey interest in the student. ✔ Provide an orientation to the assessment format. ✔ Ask additional questions [in brackets] as needed. ✔ Listen for information that will be useful to complete the assessment and later, if needed, to develop a Support Plan.

After the warm-up questions, the counselor explores seven key areas:

1. Academic functioning
2. Social functioning
3. Emotional health
4. Support network
5. Self-confidence
6. Interpersonal skills
7. Coping strategies

In each key area, the assessment follows a structured format:

- **Open-ended questions** are designed to elicit an overview of each key area in the student's own words. In the script there are primary open-ended questions to ask of every student, followed by examples of optional clarifying questions in brackets that can be used when more information is needed to understand a student response.

- **Student self-ratings** in each key area provide the counselor with more information and maintain the student in the role of expert. Self-ratings generate a great deal of information in a short period of time. Ratings are intended as a starting point for more conversation and are an efficient way for the counselor to determine where the student is functioning well and which areas may be a cause for concern. The actual numeric ratings are less important than the explanation of what each rating means to the student.

- **Targeted questions** are used by the counselor to explore any areas of concern in greater depth. A simple but helpful targeted question to use in any key area is, "Can you tell me more about that?" Targeted questions get at specifics and help to paint a more complete picture of how the student is functioning academically, socially, and emotionally. Targeted questions do not need to be asked in areas where the student is clearly functioning well.

- **A summary** concludes each key area. The counselor summarizes his or her impressions and encourages the student to confirm or correct those impressions. The counselor conveys the message that he does not want to miss any important details or get something wrong and that the student has the final word. Summarizing is a simple, effective technique used to reinforce the collaboration and ensure that the counselor has a clear understanding before moving ahead.

Key Area I: Assessment of Academic Functioning

A major focus of the EHC is to promote academic success by strengthening emotional health. The first key area explores potential sources of stress related to academic concerns, such as schoolwork, attendance, grades, or disciplinary actions. Training notes appear on the right side. What the counselor says to students appears in italics on the left with instructions in plain text. Suggestions for optional clarifying questions and prompts are also in italics, but appear in brackets.

CHECK-IN SCRIPT: OPEN-ENDED QUESTIONS ABOUT ACADEMIC FUNCTIONING	NOTES FOR THE EHC COUNSELOR
Let's talk about how things are going for you in school. How has middle school been for you so far? Optional: [*What parts do you like?* *What parts do you dislike?* *Would you say you mostly like or dislike middle school so far?*]	✔ Elicit a picture of academic adjustment ✔ Some concerns surface quickly. Others may surface later in the process.

Student ratings are an efficient way to get a great deal of information in a short period of time. The rating itself is less important than what the student means by the rating. Ask the student to give a rating for each question. Examples of optional follow-up questions are provided to give an idea of how the counselor might elicit more information in a particular area, for example, homework, bullying, or conflicts with teachers. What the counselor says to students appears in italics. Examples of optional clarifying questions are also in italics, but appear in brackets.

CHECK-IN SCRIPT: STUDENT SELF-RATING OF ACADEMIC FUNCTIONING

I'd like to ask you to help me rate a few things about school. On a scale of 1 to 6, with 1 meaning no problems or good, and 6 meaning lots of problems or bad:

	No Problems					Lots of Problems
How has your attendance been?	1	2	3	4	5	6
How about the homework? Is it too much, hard to understand? Are you keeping up?	1	2	3	4	5	6
What kinds of grades do you get?	1	2	3	4	5	6
How comfortable do you feel asking teachers for help?	1	2	3	4	5	6
How often has your behavior gotten you into trouble at school?	1	2	3	4	5	6

Optional:

[*What does a 2 mean to you?*

How many days have you missed?

How often do you get in trouble in class?

Have you ever had a detention or been suspended?

What class is giving you the most trouble?

Do you have a favorite teacher?]

There are no primary targeted questions. These questions are generated from responses to open-ended questions and student ratings. Suggestions for optional clarifying questions are in italics and appear in brackets.

CHECK-IN SCRIPT: TARGETED QUESTIONS ABOUT ACADEMIC FUNCTIONING	NOTES FOR THE EHC COUNSELOR
Optional: [*Do you ever feel like you could use help with your homework?* *In the past month, how stressed have you felt by expectations to do well or better at school?* *Can you tell me a bit more about where these high expectations are coming from?* *What is going on with your history teacher?* *Do you have trouble paying attention?*]	✔ Try to learn more about the severity and nature of problems.

The summary script includes examples of what a counselor might say to a student.

CHECK-IN SCRIPT: SUMMARY OF ACADEMIC FUNCTIONING	NOTES FOR THE EHC COUNSELOR
Examples of Summaries: ■ *From what you are saying, it sounds like things are going well. Your attendance has been great—no unexcused absences, and you are keeping up in your classes.* ■ *I'm hearing you say that you like your classes, but you are feeling overwhelmed in math and are afraid you might fail.* ■ *It sounds like you are having trouble with homework, but you don't know whom to ask for help.* *Have I got it right? Did I miss anything?*	✔ Summarize the information the student has shared about academic functioning, starting with strengths and ending with challenges. ✔ Ask the student to confirm or correct the counselor's impressions.

Key Area 2: Assessment of Social Functioning

Difficulties in social relationships can be stressful. The purpose of exploring social functioning is to understand how the student's relationships may be contributing to distress.

CHECK-IN SCRIPT: OPEN-ENDED QUESTIONS ABOUT SOCIAL FUNCTIONING	NOTES FOR THE EHC COUNSELOR
Let's talk about how things are going socially now that you are in middle school. *Do you have some friends at school you feel comfortable with?* *What do you do at lunchtime? Do you have anyone to sit with?* *Do you ever get together with friends outside of school?* Optional: [*What do you do after school?* *What do you like to do when you have free time?* *Are you in any clubs, on a sports team, or in any other group activities?* *Would you say you have a really close friend or a best friend?* *Does your best friend go to this school with you? Is she in any of your classes?*]	✔ Start with open-ended questions about peer relationships. ✔ Ask questions in an affirming way to convey that all answers are okay, whether or not a student is socially active.

CHECK-IN SCRIPT: STUDENT SELF-RATING OF SOCIAL FUNCTIONING						
Could you help me rate a few more things? On a scale of 1 to 6, with 1 being not a problem and 6 being a big problem, how much are the following things a problem for you?						
	No Problem					Big Problem
Other kids treating me unfairly, like teasing or bullying	1	2	3	4	5	6
Making friends	1	2	3	4	5	6

CHECK-IN SCRIPT: STUDENT SELF-RATING OF SOCIAL FUNCTIONING (continued)						
Having opportunities to do things with friends	1	2	3	4	5	6
Getting along with other kids	1	2	3	4	5	6

Optional:

[*What is the bully doing?*

Do any adults know?

What do you do when it happens?

What does a 2 mean to you?

What gets in the way of making friends?

What have you tried?

Can you tell me more about this?

Is this a new problem?]

CHECK-IN SCRIPT: TARGETED QUESTIONS ABOUT SOCIAL FUNCTIONING	NOTES FOR THE EHC COUNSELOR
Optional: [*Let's talk more about the bullying that is happening on the bus.* *Can you tell me more about why you think other kids don't like you?* *You say you want to stay after school for activities, but you don't know how to sign up?* *You said you don't have opportunities to do things with friends. How many days a week do you take care of your younger sister after school?* *You mentioned trouble with other kids. What kinds of trouble?*]	✔ Only ask additional questions targeted to any potential social concerns that have surfaced. For example, only ask about bullying if it was identified earlier. ✔ Try to learn more about the severity and nature of the problem.

CHECK-IN SCRIPT: SUMMARY OF SOCIAL FUNCTIONING	NOTES FOR THE EHC COUNSELOR
Examples of Summaries: • *From what you are saying, it sounds like you came to middle school with a lot of kids from your old school, and you have made some new friends.* • *It sounds like you have some friends, but no real close friends, and you would like that to be different.* • *It sounds like you are having trouble on the bus with some kids who are picking on you, and you're not sure what to do about it.* • *From what you say, you like middle school, but there are problems with kids teasing you and your friends.* • *Sounds like you would like to stay after school for activities, but your mom doesn't like that idea because you will get home too late to do your homework.* *Did I miss anything? Did I get it right?*	✔ Summarize information the student has shared about social functioning, starting with strengths and ending with challenges. ✔ Ask the student to confirm or correct the counselor's impressions.

Key Area 3: Assessment of Emotional Functioning

Students are often riding a roller coaster of emotions. The emotional functioning key area explores how emotions or the inability to manage them may be related to the student's distress and adjustment to middle school. The questions about emotional functioning are placed at this later stage of the Check-In because they are the most personal questions asked. The goal is that students will be ready to talk more openly about sensitive areas once they have had time to get comfortable with the EHC counselor.

The emotional functioning key area is formatted slightly differently from the academic and social functioning areas. Because the student has already rated areas of emotional functioning on the MFQ during classroom screening, there is no need to self-rate again. Instead, the EHC counselor reviews the ratings from the MFQ to begin the assessment of emotional functioning. The counselor should keep in mind that the student may feel differently than on Screening Day.

CHECK-IN SCRIPT: INTRODUCE THE KEY AREA OF EMOTIONAL FUNCTIONING	NOTES FOR THE EHC COUNSELOR
Thanks for sharing about school and friends. Now I want to ask you more about how you have been feeling lately, because the questionnaire you filled out on Screening Day indicated that you may be feeling down or stressed. I'd like to understand more about how you are feeling and how we can work to help you feel happier and less stressed.	✔ Convey that all feelings are okay and talking about feelings can be helpful.
CHECK-IN SCRIPT: OPEN-ENDED QUESTIONS: USE RATINGS FROM THE MFQ	**NOTES FOR THE EHC COUNSELOR**
When you filled out the screening questionnaire in class, you said that you were *[feeling lonely* *crying a lot* *felt like nothing was any fun anymore.]* *Can you tell me how you have been feeling lately?*	✔ Before the Check-In, review the student's MFQ. ✔ Plan in advance to use one or two MFQ items as an introduction to the open-ended questions.

The EHC counselor asks targeted questions about several aspects of emotional functioning that get at feelings of depression, anxiety, and low self-esteem, all of which factor into the overall emotional functioning of the student. Ask the targeted questions in each section. Depending on the answers to these questions, ask optional clarifying questions, in brackets, to clarify or expand on a response. There is no need to ask every optional question, and you may use others as needed. These are suggestions.

CHECK-IN SCRIPT: TARGETED QUESTIONS ABOUT EMOTIONAL FUNCTIONING	NOTES FOR THE EHC COUNSELOR
So, would you say that you have been feeling mostly happy or mostly sad? Optional: *[Do you find you have days where you feel down and days when you feel okay, or are all the days feeling like down days right now?* *What things make you feel unhappy?* *How would others know when you are sad?* *What makes you happy again when you feel unhappy?]*	✔ The conversation to assess for signs of depression is approached in a broad way with the first question.
How about feeling annoyed? Do you ever feel irritated even at little things? Optional: *[Do you lose your temper a lot?* *Would you say you have a hot temper?]*	✔ Irritability is a symptom of depression that can interfere with academic and social functioning.
Some kids tell me they feel lonely, and I wonder if you ever feel this way. Optional: *[How often do you feel this way?* *Is this a change since you started middle school, or have you felt this way for a long time?]*	✔ When teens isolate themselves, it can be a symptom of depression. ✔ Isolation can also worsen depression.
Do you have trouble sleeping? Like getting to sleep, waking up in the night, or waking up too early in the morning? Optional: *[How often do you have trouble sleeping?* *How much sleep do you usually get at night?* *What time do you usually go to sleep?* *What time do you usually get up on school days?]*	✔ Changes in sleep patterns can be a symptom of depression. ✔ When teens do not get enough sleep, they are at risk of emotional health problems.

CHECK-IN SCRIPT: TARGETED QUESTIONS ABOUT EMOTIONAL FUNCTIONING (continued)	NOTES FOR THE EHC COUNSELOR
How about eating? Have you been eating more or less than usual? Optional: [*Would your parents say they are worried about your eating habits?* *Have you lost or gained weight lately?* *What do you eat for breakfast?* *What do you eat for lunch?]*	✔ Changes in eating patterns can be a symptom of depression. ✔ Students who skip breakfast have less energy for academics.
Middle school kids can get down on themselves. Does that ever happen to you? Optional: [*If you could, what would you change about yourself?* *What would you keep the same?* *How would you describe your strengths and weaknesses?]*	✔ Distressed teens see themselves through a lens of negativity. This can impact self-esteem and feelings of self-worth.
Everyone worries sometimes. What do you worry about? *On a scale of 1 to 10, how worried have you felt in the past month?* Optional: [*Is there anything going on at school that we have not talked about?* *Is there anything stressing you out at home or in the community?* *Does anyone else share your worries?* *Does anyone else know how worried you are?]*	✔ This question may feel repetitive. It is asked to at this point to intentionally provide another opportunity to evaluate distress once the student may be more comfortable with the Check-In.

The assessment of key areas of functioning is complete and the next script summarizes what the counselor has learned about the student's functioning in all three key areas.

CHECK-IN SCRIPT: SUMMARY OF ACADEMIC, SOCIAL, AND EMOTIONAL FUNCTIONING	NOTES FOR THE EHC COUNSELOR
Examples of Summaries: *From what you are saying, it sounds as if you like middle school, but there are some things going on that are getting you down.* *It sounds like you are not getting along very well with your math teacher. It's starting to make you feel bad and anxious about going to that class.* *From what you say, you are feeling kind of lonely. It's been hard to make new friends, and that is really getting you down.* *I'm concerned that you are having a lot of trouble getting to sleep at night and aren't getting enough rest to do your best in class.* *Did I hear you correctly? Did I miss anything?*	✔ Summarize the information about emotional functioning. Start with strengths and end with challenges. ✔ Integrate what the student has conveyed previously about academic and social key areas.

This completes the questions that give the EHC counselor a picture of the student's academic, social, and emotional stressors. The next section turns attention to two pieces of the strengths puzzle: the student's support network and level of self-confidence.

Key Areas 4 and 5:
Assessment of Support Network and Level of Self-Confidence

A strong support network and a high level of self-confidence are two pieces of the strengths puzzle that may help students manage stress before it turns to distress.

CHECK-IN SCRIPT: SUPPORT	NOTES FOR THE EHC COUNSELOR
I'd like to ask you a few questions about the kind of support you are getting. *How often can you turn to your family for help when something is bothering you?* *How about other adults who could help you if you needed it, like relatives, neighbors, or family friends?* *How about at school—if something was bothering you, what adult at school could you turn to for help?* *In the last year, have you seen someone like a counselor, doctor, or maybe a person at your place of worship because you were feeling stressed?* Optional: *[Who in the family would you turn to first?* *Who else could you go to in the family?* *Are you still getting support from this counselor?* *How often?* *Is it easy to get time with the people who support you when you want someone to talk with?]*	✔ Ask these questions in a way that conveys that any answer is okay, even if the student does do not have any support.

CHECK-IN SCRIPT: SELF-CONFIDENCE

We've been talking about the kinds of problems and stressors that can come up in middle school. I'm curious. On a scale of 1 to 10, with 1 being not confident and 10 being the most confident middle school student, how confident do you feel that you can handle your problems?

Not very confident									Very confident
1	2	3	4	5	6	7	8	9	10

And overall, I'm wondering how well you would say you are adjusting to middle school so far. On a scale of 1 to 10, where 1 is a very poor adjustment and 10 is a very good adjustment, how would you rate your adjustment?

Very poor									Very good
1	2	3	4	5	6	7	8	9	10

I'm curious. Where would you like your adjustment to be on the scale of 1 to 10 in a month from now?

Very poor									Very good
1	2	3	4	5	6	7	8	9	10

Optional targeted questions are asked to expand the answers to the three ratings of confidence asked above.

CHECK-IN SCRIPT: TARGETED QUESTIONS ABOUT SELF-CONFIDENCE	NOTES FOR THE EHC COUNSELOR
Optional: [*So you are at a 6 and would like to be an 8.* *What would things look like if you were at an 8?* *How can we get you from a 2 to a 5?*]	✔ Only ask additional questions targeted to any potential concerns about self-confidence.

CHECK-IN SCRIPT: SUMMARY OF SUPPORT AND CONFIDENCE	NOTES FOR THE EHC COUNSELOR
Examples: *It seems like you have a lot of people you can count on to help you when you are feeling stressed or having a problem.* *You seem really confident that you can tackle problems.* *From what you say, you feel close to a lot of people, but they aren't always around when you need them. Sometimes you feel confident, but not at school.* *You seem to have a lot of confidence. However, I'm thinking that it might help to get a few adults involved to help with your concerns.* *Have I got it right? Did I miss anything?*	✔ Pause to summarize impressions about the support network and the assessment of the self-confidence. ✔ Ask the student to confirm or correct your impressions.

Key Areas 6 and 7:
Assessment of Interpersonal Skills and Coping Strategies

There are no direct questions about interpersonal skills and coping strategies. The counselor learns about these key areas through observation. Throughout the Check-In, the counselor listens and watches for these two pieces of the student puzzle, taking note of how skilled the student is at communicating and whether he reports using effective coping strategies to solve problems and manage feelings. The counselor's observations will complete the inventory of external and internal resources that equip the student to manage distress. The counselor is now prepared for the next activity, deciding whether or not a student needs a Support Plan.

Fourth Activity: Determine Whether a Support Plan Is Needed

The EHC counselor synthesizes the Check-In information and decides if there is a need for additional support. The counselor is weighing strengths versus distress in each area of concern. The counselor draws on experience and judgment to formulate a picture of each student's strengths puzzle. Students who need academic support are generally stressed about grades or workloads and are usually quite accurate in their assessments of gaps in their abilities to meet academic expectations. Students who need social support are usually clear about the distress they feel related to their inability to make friends, resolve social conflicts, or deal with bullies and peer pressure.

Decisions about students who need emotional support may be fairly simple. Some students are clearly struggling with situational stressors such as a parental divorce or the military deployment of a sibling. They may have witnessed community violence and have clear-cut symptoms of post-traumatic stress.

Other decisions about students who need emotional support are less straightforward. Some students may appear to have an academic or social concern that turns out to be an emotional concern. While asking targeted questions in the emotional key area, it becomes clear that what seems like a homework or peer group problem is really signaling low self-esteem, depression, or anxiety. For example, a counselor who meets with a B student who can't shake worries about grades or a well-liked student who constantly puts himself down may at first think there is an academic or social concern. The other not so straightforward situation is when a student has an emotional concern in combination with academic and social needs.

The decision-making process is organized into a grid that serves as visual aid to help the student understand why the counselor is recommending a plan or not.

SUPPORT PLAN DECISION GRID			
AREA	MARK EACH AREA	ADEQUATE STRENGTHS AND RESOURCES IN PLACE TO ADDRESS CONCERNS?	NEED PLAN?
Academic Is there a concern? YES or NO	What is going well: What is not going well:	What supports are in place? Adequate to address concern? YES or NO	YES or NO
Social Is there a concern? YES or NO	What is going well: What is not going well:	What supports are in place? Adequate to address concern? YES or NO	YES or NO
Emotional Is there a concern? YES or NO	What is going well: What is not going well:	What supports are in place? Adequate to address concern? YES or NO	YES or NO
Other Is there a concern? YES or NO	What is going well: What is not going well:	What supports are in place? Adequate to address concern? YES or NO	YES or NO

The counselor fills out the grid with brief notes, incorporating language the student used during the Check-In. The student makes sure the grid is accurate. Once the counselor and the student have agreed upon the content, they have a common map to guide their decision making. Below are three grids. The first grid gives an example of how the academic area of the grid might look for a student who needs a plan. The second grid depicts a student who has an academic concern but does not need a plan. Finally, the third grid gives an example of a student with an emotional concern.

SUPPORT PLAN DECISION GRID: ACADEMICS			
AREA	MARK EACH AREA	ADEQUATE STRENGTHS AND RESOURCES IN PLACE TO ADDRESS CONCERNS? LIST	NEED PLAN?
Academic Is there a concern? ✔YES or NO	What is going well: *Joe is trying hard.* *Joe wants to do well.* What is not going well: *Joe is not turning in assignments in math.* *Joe failed the social studies exam.*	What supports are in place? *Joe asked a friend for help before the social studies exam.* Adequate to address concern? YES or ✔NO	✔YES or NO

SUPPORT PLAN DECISION GRID: ACADEMICS			
AREA	MARK EACH AREA	ADEQUATE STRENGTHS AND RESOURCES IN PLACE TO ADDRESS CONCERNS? LIST	NEED PLAN?
Academic Is there a concern? ✔YES or NO	What is going well: *Chiu told her mother about her homework problems.* What is not going well: *Chiu does not complete all sections of homework assignments, getting only partial credit. Chiu daydreams in class and does not hear all instructions.*	What supports are in place? *Mother recently bought Chiu a planner and now reviews it nightly. Chiu asked her brother to help with homework that she does not understand.* Adequate to address concern? ✔YES or NO	YES or ✔NO

SUPPORT PLAN DECISION GRID: EMOTIONAL			
AREA	MARK EACH AREA	ADEQUATE STRENGTHS AND RESOURCES IN PLACE TO ADDRESS CONCERNS? LIST	NEED PLAN?
Emotional Is there a concern? ✔YES or NO	What is going well: *Jay says he told his father he is worried.* What is not going well: *Jay is having trouble sleeping. He overslept and missed school several times. It is hard to concentrate in class. He is worried about grades and his grandmother, who is sick.*	What supports are in place? *Jay's father told him to go to bed earlier and not to worry about his grandmother.* Adequate to address concern? YES or ✔NO	✔YES or NO

Once the grid is filled out, the counselor summarizes the content. This serves as an overall review of the key areas of concern as well as the key areas of strength. The scripts below are examples of summaries in one of the key areas of concern that might be used with Joe, Chiu, or Jay.

FOLLOW-UP SCRIPT: SUMMARY OF KEY AREAS	NOTES FOR THE EHC COUNSELOR

Joe:
 	
We have talked about many areas of your life, school, friends, and how you are feeling. Let's look at the grid and I'll summarize what I think I have learned from our talk. From what you shared with me, you are working really hard and want to do well in classes, but you are pretty worried about how you are doing in math. You are having trouble getting your assignments in on time and you recently failed a big social studies test. Have I got it right? You asked a friend for help, but that wasn't enough.
 	
Chiu:
 	
Sounds like your biggest concern is how things are going in math. You have missed some assignments and don't always hear the teacher's instructions. I'm really impressed that you shared your concerns with your mom. Sounds like the two of you have a great plan for tackling the problem. You mentioned she got you a planner and reviews it with you every night. Also, your brother is willing to help when you need it. Seems like this support will get you on track soon. What do you think?
 	
Jay:
 	
Thanks for filling me in on how you are doing. It seems like you are really worried about your grandmother, and that is making it hard to get enough sleep and concentrate in class. Then these problems are causing you to worry about your grades and attendance. The stress seems to be really piling up. I'm glad you have shared your worries with your father. Keep that up and maybe we can also find additional things to help you feel less stressed. How does that sound? Have I missed anything?
	✔ Summarize impressions of three key areas of potential concern.
	
	✔ Summarize the three key areas of strength:
	
	  1. Who is in the support network and available to help?
	  2. What skills are observed or talked about by student?
	  3. What is observed level of student's self-confidence?
	
	✔ Check perceptions to make sure counselor and student are in agreement and are not overlooking anything important. This is critical before deciding whether or not there is a need for a Support Plan.

A concern in any key area that is not being adequately addressed signals the need for a Support Plan.

Matrix for Determining Need for Support Plan		
	Is there a concern? NO	Is there a concern? YES
Is current support adequate? YES	No Support Plan is needed	No Support Plan is needed
Is current support adequate? NO	No Support Plan is needed	SUPPORT PLAN IS NEEDED

After the Support Plan decision has been made, the Check-In will follow one of two pathways. One pathway is taken when no Support Plan is needed. The first step on this pathway is for the student and counselor to discuss the phone call the counselor will make to the parent. The other pathway is for students who need a Support Plan. The first step on this pathway is for the counselor and the student to discuss the need for a Support Plan. Here are sample scripts for each pathway.

EXAMPLE OF SUMMARY FOR STUDENTS WHO **DO NOT NEED** A SUPPORT PLAN	EXAMPLE OF SUMMARY FOR STUDENTS WHO **NEED** A SUPPORT PLAN
Based on what you have told me, it seems that things are going well and you feel confident that, if you keep using the support you are getting from your family and teachers, you'll be on track for a good year. The fact that you have been communicating with your teachers seems to be helping. Does that match with how you see yourself, or do you think you need some additional support? *Great. Let's talk about how I can communicate that to your parent. . . .*	*Based on what you have told me, I think that things could really improve for you if you got some extra support with your schoolwork. I'm also thinking that you will be happier here in middle school if we can find ways for you to meet some kids and have fun outside class. Seems like it has been hard to talk to your teachers or your mom about your worries. Does that match how you are feeling? I have some ideas that have helped other kids in your situation. Is it all right if we talk about some ideas now?*

At this point, the counselor discusses the call home with students who do not need a Support Plan and excuses them to go back to class. Students who need a Support Plan will continue to work with the counselor to draft a plan that will later be shared with a parent during the Parent Phone Call.

Chapter 10

Developing a Student Support Plan

When there is a need for additional support, the EHC counselor works with the student to create a Support Plan. By instilling hope and encouraging students to come up with their own solutions, the counselor fosters student investment in the process. The plan will have a higher likelihood of being implemented if the student is an active participant in its development, has a full understanding of its elements, and is clear about how it could help.

How to Develop a Support Plan

The development of the Support Plan includes four activities:

1. Introduce the plan and brainstorm ideas (5 minutes).
2. Evaluate ideas and draft a plan (5 minutes).
3. Check for barriers and confirm a plan (5 minutes).
4. Discuss the Parent Phone Call (5 minutes).

FIRST ACTIVITY: INTRODUCE AND BRAINSTORM

The EHC counselor introduces the idea that having a plan can lead to positive changes for the student. Problems can seem overwhelming. Talking about goals and creating a written plan help to ensure that the counselor and student are moving in the same direction. The student is reassured that creating a plan and breaking it down into small, doable steps can make problems easier to handle.

CHECK-IN SCRIPT: INTRODUCE THE SUPPORT PLAN	NOTES FOR THE EHC COUNSELOR
I know lots of students who have been stressed out in middle school and have gotten help to feel better. I'm meeting with many students in the next few weeks to figure out what kinds of additional support might be helpful. I think you and I should work together on a plan. A plan will give us a road map to help you get on track to do your best in middle school.	✔ Reassure student that having problems and asking for help is normal. ✔ Emphasize that the student is not alone in needing help. ✔ Instill a sense of hope that things can get better.

A brief brainstorming session is used to create a list of ideas called a menu of options. The EHC counselor and student think of all the ideas they can to tackle each identified concern. The EHC resource list can be consulted to spark ideas for the menu. The resulting list, individualized for each student, includes options to build on the student's strengths, strengthen his support network, and lead to the development of new skills and coping strategies. Creating a menu communicates the message that many roads lead to improved emotional health.

CHECK-IN SCRIPT: BRAINSTORMING	NOTES FOR THE EHC COUNSELOR
There are lots of ways to solve problems. Let's think of all the ideas we can that might help with your concerns, because having a plan can really help. Let's start with the first concern. What do you think might help with getting your homework done and turned in? Let's think of as many ideas as we can before we decide which one to try. Optional questions to facilitate brainstorming: [*Are you aware of any support that is available at school?* *Who might be able to help you with your concerns?* *Let's think about ideas you think might work for you to help with your adjustment to middle school.* *What has worked for your friends or siblings?* *May I tell you about the supports that are available here at school so you can see what you think?*]	✔ Explain rationale for brainstorming. ✔ Create a list of ideas and call it the menu of options. ✔ Represent current supports and new ideas. ✔ Encourage as many ideas as possible. Suspend judgment and do not evaluate ideas until there is a complete list.

To illustrate the outcome of a brainstorming session, the chart below includes a menu of options for Lee, a student who scored high for signs of distress on the MFQ. Lee is having trouble keeping up with the academic demands of middle school and spending many hours each night on homework, which leaves her tired and anxious. She does not have the energy to make new friends and is feeling lonely. She does not share her distress with her mother because she does not want to worry her.

The EHC counselor discusses the rationale for developing a Support Plan and together, she and Lee brainstorm a Menu of Options with ideas for each concern on her list. To generate a long list of options, the counselor encourages all ideas without evaluating them.

If a student gets stuck during the brainstorming process and cannot think of ideas, the counselor has several ways to facilitate the process. The counselor contributes an idea to get the ball rolling or suggests that they take turns providing ideas. One technique is called "best friend." In this technique, the student is asked, "What would your best friend recommend you try?" or "What would a friend try if she were having this problem?"

Lee and the counselor brainstorm and write the following Menu of Options:

CONCERN: WORRIED ABOUT GRADES Ideas for academic support	• *Attend the homework club* • *Find a private tutor* • *Use online resources* • *Ask a teacher for help* • *Ask older brother or mother for help*
CONCERN: FEELING LONELY Ideas for social support	• *Join an after-school activity* • *Look into activities or classes at the community center* • *Get together with old friends* • *Try out the youth group at church* • *Sign up for a social skills group with the school counselor* • *Take the school activity list home to show Mom*
CONCERN: FEELING TIRED AND DOWN Ideas for emotional support	• *Talk with Mom about worries* • *Set up a time to talk with the school counselor* • *Get a referral to a community mental health counselor* • *Talk to the youth director at church* • *Call up favorite aunt to talk*

SECOND ACTIVITY: EVALUATE OPTIONS AND DRAFT A PLAN

Once they have generated a solid menu, the EHC counselor guides the student to evaluate the pros and cons of each idea on the menu. The counselor asks about the positive and negative aspects of each idea to find out which ones may have the most success and which the student is really willing to try.

CHECK-IN SCRIPT: EVALUATE OPTIONS AND DRAFT A PLAN	NOTES FOR THE EHC COUNSELOR
Let's take a look at each idea and think about what might be help-ful about the idea and what might be a problem. This will help you decide if you want to add it to your plan. Optional: [*What do you think will work?* *What do you like about this idea?* *What don't you like about this idea?* *What is the idea you think will work best? Least? Why? Why not?*]	✔ Address the helpful and unhelpful aspects of each idea. ✔ Let the student do the evaluating.

The Check-In script has a space for listing the pros and cons for ideas. The counselor makes notes on the list with Lee:

CONCERN:	IDEAS:	PROS:	CONS/BARRIERS:
1. Worried about grades	Mom will sign me up for the after-school homework club. I will go to lunchtime home-work help. I will ask my brother to help me. I will ask a friend for help.	I know someone who goes. I want to try it. I might have more free time after school. My brother is good at math. I like my friends.	I'd miss practice. I would need transportation. I will not have free time at lunch. My brother has his own homework. It's embarrassing. They don't have time.
2. Feeling lonely	I will ask someone to eat lunch with me. Call an old friend and get together.	I wouldn't be so lonely. I want to see my friend.	The person might say no. I might be too tired. She might be busy.

CONCERN:	IDEAS:	PROS:	CONS/BARRIERS:
3. Feeling tired and down	I will agree to an earlier bedtime. Meet the school counselor.	Mom could help. Might help to know the counselor.	I like staying up late. Not sure this will help. I would be embarrassed.

After the review of pros and cons, the student selects ideas to put on the Support Plan. The counselor gives input and may need to gently nudge the student toward practical solutions, but ultimately the student will decide what he or she is willing to try. Lee's plan should be realistic and consist of actions that Lee agrees to take. A plan has a greater chance of success if each action on the plan and its timeline for completion are very clear. It is important that everyone involved understands what actions will be taken and who is responsible for taking action. Lee's plan includes specifics about when she will talk with her mother, how many days a week she will ask her brother for help, and when the EHC counselor will schedule a meeting with the school counselor.

The following is the draft Support Plan that Lee and the ECH counselor confirm:

CONCERN:	PLAN:	
1. Worried about grades	1a. On the phone call, EHC counselor will give Lee's mother the phone number so she can enroll Lee in the after-school homework club. Lee will attend the homework club two times a week.	1b. Lee will ask tonight if her brother can spend a half hour two or three times a week helping her with math homework.
2. Feeling lonely	2a. Lee will ask her friend Asa to hang out this weekend.	2b. EHC counselor will talk with Mom about options for getting Lee together with old friends.
3. Feeling tired and down	3a. EHC counselor will introduce Lee to the school counselor after confirming this is okay with Mom.	3b. Lee agrees to an earlier bedtime. The EHC counselor will discuss sleep ideas with Mom during the parent phone call.

THIRD ACTIVITY: CHECK FOR BARRIERS AND CONFIRM THE PLAN

The final activity to complete before confirming a plan is to check for any barriers that might get in the way of the plan. The counselor helps the student identify and problem solve solutions to specific barriers. During this review, it might become apparent that a part of the plan is not going to work and should be set aside.

The counselor asks the student about both external and internal barriers. External barriers are sometimes called logistical barriers and include things like lack of transportation, cost, or an inconvenient location. Internal barriers, also known as perceptual barriers, include attitudes, feelings, or beliefs, such as believing that a solution will not help, being afraid of what others might think, or feeling like help is not really necessary. Either type of barrier can defeat a plan, so both are addressed with the student and later with the parent.

CHECK-IN SCRIPT: CHECK FOR BARRIERS AND CONFIRM A DRAFT PLAN	NOTES FOR THE EHC COUNSELOR
Before we decide for sure what to keep on the plan, let's think about things that might get in the way. Optional: [*What might get in the way of this idea working?* *Are there any logistical reasons like lack of transportation or registration fees that might cause this plan to fail?* *Are there any parts of the plan that you don't really think will help or maybe you don't really want to try?* *Are there any reasons you or your parent might not believe that this idea would work?* *You say you don't have a ride home. Is there any means of transportation that you could use to get home from the after-school class?*]	✔ Anticipate both external and internal barriers. ✔ If barriers are identified, think through how to overcome them or remove the idea from the plan.

Common barriers a student might report include:

LOGISTICAL BARRIERS	PERCEPTUAL BARRIERS
Help is too expensive.	A lack of confidence that the support will be helpful.
No appointments except during school and work hours.	Has had negative experience with helpers in the past.
Services are too far away or inconvenient.	Afraid of what family or friends will say.
Do not know how to contact the service or person.	Gets discouraged trying to find people to help.
There is no way to get there.	Does not want to try it.
There is a long wait for appointments.	Thinks problems are not serious.
There are language barriers or cultural concerns.	Wants to handle problems on own.

Once Lee and the counselor have reviewed potential barriers, they are ready to finalize a plan.

OPTIONAL ACTIVITY: ADDRESS PERCEPTUAL BARRIERS WITH MOTIVATIONAL STRATEGIES

The EHC counselor guides a process that has enabled students to consider options and envision actions that might help to relieve their distress. At this point in the process, some students are hesitant to take action. If needed, the EHC counselor incorporates empirically supported approaches from the science of behavior change to address student reluctance (Rollnick & Miller, 1995; Hettema, Steele, & Miller, 2005). The counselor decides how to light a spark of enthusiasm for each hesitant student by drawing upon one or more strategies. An EHC pilot study documented that a significantly higher percentage of students with Support Plans that had been developed using motivational strategies were successfully linked to recommended supports, compared to students whose Support Plans did not include the use of these strategies (McCormick et al., 2009).

STRATEGY: CHECK ON OWNERSHIP OF THE PLAN.

- *Do we have a plan that you feel okay about?*

- *What would you add or take out so you could feel good about the plan?*

STRATEGY: RATE READINESS TO TRY THE PLAN.

- *Let's rate how ready you are to try the plan. On a scale of 1 to 10, where 1 is not ready and 10 is very ready, how ready do you feel to do the things we have listed on the plan?*

Not ready									Very ready
1	2	3	4	5	6	7	8	9	10

- *Why did you give that number?*

- *What would make it higher?*

- *So, you say you are at a 3. What would help you get ready to try the plan?*

STRATEGY: RATE CONFIDENCE IN THE PLAN.

- *On a scale of 1 to 10, where 1 is not confident and 10 is very confident, how confident are you that the plan we have discussed will help you?*

Not confident									Very confident
1	2	3	4	5	6	7	8	9	10

- *Why did you give your confidence that number?*

- *What would make it higher?*

- *What would have to happen to move the number up a notch?*

STRATEGY: EXPLORE HESITANCY WITHOUT RATING.

- *What would help make you ready to try the plan?*

- *You are thinking that you might not need help right now. How would you know that it was time to do something about your distress?*

- *You seem hesitant. Let's think how we can rework the plan to make it fit better for you.*

FOURTH ACTIVITY: DISCUSS THE PARENT PHONE CALL

Once the plan is finalized, the EHC counselor expresses confidence in both the plan and the student's ability to execute it. Next comes a discussion of how and when to communicate the plan to the parent. The parent plays an important role in fine-tuning and carrying out the Support Plan.

The EHC counselor reminds the student about the Parent Phone Call, asks for contact information, and then models for the student what she would like to say to the parent. She uses wording that is optimistic and strength based and delivers reassurance that the student is not in trouble. This is the moment when the counselor asks the student if the message is okay, and the counselor and student negotiate exactly how the plan will be conveyed to the parent.

CHECK-IN SCRIPT: DISCUSS THE PARENT PHONE CALL	NOTES FOR THE EHC COUNSELOR
Let's talk about next steps. Remember I told you that I will connect with your parent after we meet today? Would you like me to talk to your mother or your father or to a different caregiver? *Will I need a translator?* **[If yes]** *What is his first language?* *What number should I use to reach your parent?* *Are there good times to reach your parent?*	✔ Find out from the student whom to contact and how to reach that person by phone.

Example:	✔ Suggest wording to be used in parent phone call.
Here's what I would like to say during the call to your parent. I want to make sure it sounds okay to you. First, I will say to your mother:	
"Thanks for letting Lee participate in the EHC. She filled out a questionnaire in social studies class last week and then missed her gym class to meet with me today."	✔ Start with a thank-you to the parent and a reminder about the EHC.
Then I am going to tell her about your strengths and the concerns we discussed. I'd like to say, "Lee is a great kid, and I really enjoyed talking with her. It seems like many things are going well for her at middle school. Her attendance has been great. She is working very hard to get all her schoolwork done on time, and she even had the courage to ask a friend for extra help."	✔ Review strengths and what is going well.
Is it okay to say all that?	✔ Listen for student's affirmation.
After that, I want to let her know that you are feeling stressed about keeping up in math. You are not doing as well as you would like. You stay up late to do homework and work so hard that you are tired a lot and missing out on fun with friends. That's making you feel lonely.	✔ Review concerns.
Is it okay to say all that?	✔ Review the plan and reinforce that potential solutions came from collaborating with the student.
I'll let her know that we have some ideas for helping you. You said you would like to try the homework club and also want some help from your brother. We talked about you getting more sleep, and I'm going to talk with her about that. I'll share that you are willing to talk with her to set up a new bedtime. I'll tell her that you want to get together with Asa and may need transportation. Last, you think it might help for me to introduce you to the school counselor so that you know who to go to at school when you need support.	
Is all that okay to share with your mother?	✔ Confirm the wording with the student.
Is it okay with you if I say it that way?	
Is there anything else you would want me to say to her?	✔ Negotiate any concerns about wording until you come to agreement.

STUDENTS WHO DO NOT WANT TO SHARE CONCERNS WITH PARENTS

When the counselor conveys a supportive, upbeat message, most students will agree with the wording for the call to the parent. Sometimes a student will want to add something or edit the wording. On a rare occasion, a student does not want the counselor to talk with a parent. In this case, the counselor reminds the student that they discussed the call home at the beginning of the Check-In and, at the very least, the call will include a thank-you to the parent for letting the student participate and the message that the student missed a class for the Check-In. If anything else is conveyed to the parent, it will be decided together.

The counselor reminds the student that one of the benefits of the call home is that the parent gets a positive report about the student. Most students will agree to the sharing of positive feedback.

Parents often hear about problems from the school but not about how well a student is doing. I want to give you some recognition for your hard work and for the things that are going well so far in middle school. This is a chance for me to brag about you. Does that make sense?

The counselor discusses the benefits of letting parents know about the student's concerns. It is a time to remind students that help is available, and parents and others can support them to get help. Parents may need to provide transportation, pay registration fees, or support the plan in other ways.

I can see that you are hesitant for me to talk to your parent. It can help when your parent knows what is bothering you. Parents can support students and help them solve problems. Your mother may be able to drive you to your friend's house this weekend and sign your permission form for the homework club. Joining the club has a fee, and your mother may be willing to pay for that if she knows you really want to try it out.

The counselor takes as much time as necessary to sort out the student's reluctance and work out an agreement for the parent call. Ultimately, if a student does not want the counselor to share information, the counselor calls to thank the parent. She encourages the parent to ask the student about his or her experience with the EHC. When a parent asks the student about how he or she experienced the Check-In, it can open the door to communication and provide an opportunity for the student and parent to discuss concerns directly.

Chapter 11

Connecting With Parents

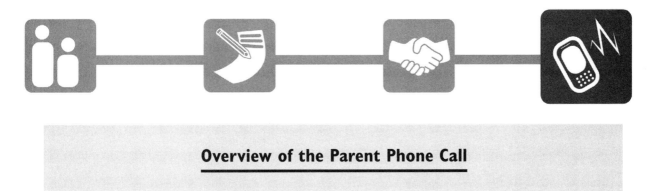

Overview of the Parent Phone Call

At the completion of the Student Check-In, the focus of the EHC shifts from school to home. The EHC is based on a collaborative model, and during the Parent Phone Call the counselor has the opportunity to forge a partnership with the parent. During the call, the counselor reminds parents about the EHC and asks for their expert perspective on the how the student is adjusting to middle school. The role of the counselor is to share information, solicit feedback, offer encouragement and support, and facilitate implementation of the Support Plan. The counselor follows the phone script and has in hand a copy of the student Decision Grid and Support Plan.

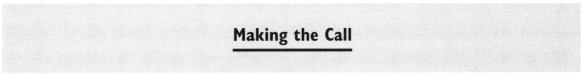

Making the Call

In the brief Parent Phone Call, the EHC counselor engages the parent in seven activities that follow in quick succession.

FIRST ACTIVITY: INTRODUCTION

The counselor begins the call with a reminder about the EHC. Parents, who often keep track of a multitude of details about multiple family members, may or may not recall that the child has participated. The counselor may be perceived as an outsider calling to report personal information. Thus, it is important to reorient parents to the EHC and why they are receiving this phone call.

PHONE SCRIPT: INTRODUCTION	**NOTES FOR THE EHC COUNSELOR**
Hello. My name is **[name]**, *and I am on the Emotional Health Checkup team at Lee's middle school. Is this a good time to talk for a few minutes about Lee and the Emotional Health Checkup?*	✔ Introduce yourself. ✔ If it is not a good time to talk, ask parent for a better time.
First, I wanted to remind you that the EHC is a program that involves all students during the transition to middle school and is designed to help students who are stressed. We know that starting middle school can be stressful, and the EHC program tries to give a helping hand to students who need extra support so that they can have a positive middle school experience. *We find that if we can identify concerns early, we can help students get connected to supports that will reduce the chance that problems will get worse and interfere with their adjustment to middle school.*	✔ Give a brief recap of the EHC.
Thank you for letting Lee participate in the program. Last week she filled out the questionnaire, and Lee's answers on the questionnaire showed some signs of stress. I met with Lee today to talk about how things are going at school with classes and friends and how she has been feeling lately. Lee agreed that I could share some feedback about what I learned and check in about how you feel her transition to middle school is going so far. Is that okay?	✔ Thank the parent and review the student's involvement in the EHC to date.
First of all, Lee seems like a great kid, and I really enjoyed talking with her. She is working hard and wants to do well in middle school. In general, there are many things going well for her. *I realize that I only had a brief amount of time with Lee and that, as her parent, you are the real expert. . . .*	✔ Share strengths using the language that you and the student agreed upon. ✔ Communicate that the parent is the expert.

SECOND ACTIVITY: SHARE FEEDBACK AND SOLICIT PARENT PERSPECTIVE

The EHC counselor shares a summary of the student's adjustment to middle school and solicits the parent's views. There are two types of phone call scripts to use at this stage. The first script is for the conversation with parents of students who do not need a plan.

PHONE SCRIPT: FEEDBACK FOR PARENT WHEN NO PLAN IS NEEDED	NOTES FOR THE EHC COUNSELOR
From what your son shared with me, he seems to be adjusting well, and I really do not have any concerns about his transition to middle school. Does that match how you are feeling about his adjustment? How is it going from your point of view?	✔ Report your disposition of no plan needed. ✔ Solicit parent's perspective.

If the parent agrees that there are no concerns, the counselor thanks the parent for his or her time and perspective, encourages the parent to check in regularly with the student about how school is going, and ends the call.

Parents have reported that the EHC parent phone call was the first time they had received a call from school with an optimistic report about their son or daughter. As an unforeseen by-product of the EHC, these calls have often played a role in establishing or strengthening positive relationships between parents and schools.

The second script is used with parents when their child has drafted a Support Plan.

PHONE SCRIPT: FEEDBACK FOR PARENT WHEN THERE IS A SUPPORT PLAN	NOTES FOR THE EHC COUNSELOR
Even though there are many things going well for Lee, I also had a few concerns after talking with her. She says she is feeling stressed about her math grade and keeping up with her assignments. She also said she is staying up very late to finish homework and thus is often tired at school. She is also missing friends and feeling lonely. *Does what I reported about Lee match how you are feeling about her adjustment to middle school?* *Did I get it right?* **Example** of responses to parent input: *We really match up on how we are seeing things for Lee right now. Except I also hear you saying that Lee is trying really hard, but you have other concerns because she seems really moody and you heard from your neighbor that kids are picking on her on the bus.*	✔ Use the language that you and the student agreed upon. ✔ Share your concerns about the student's middle school transition. ✔ Solicit parent's perspective. ✔ Summarize parent concerns. Use any wording introduced by the parent.

THIRD ACTIVITY: SHARE THE SUPPORT PLAN

The focus of the phone call shifts to supports.

PHONE SCRIPT: SHARING THE SUPPORT PLAN	NOTES FOR THE EHC COUNSELOR
Lee and I talked about what might help her feel less stressed, and we came up with some ideas that she thought might work. *She said she would like to try the after-school homework club two days a week to get extra help with her math homework.* *She also thought that her brother might be able to help her with homework for a half hour a few days a week.* *She agreed that setting an earlier bedtime may help her get more sleep, and she thought you could help her get to bed on time.* *She thinks that meeting the school counselor is a good idea in case she needs to talk to an adult at school. I would be happy to introduce her to the counselor, if that's okay with you.* *How does the plan sound from your point of view?* *You mentioned problems on the bus. Is there anything you would like to add to the plan?*	✔ Share the plan using the language agreed upon with the student. ✔ Address any new concerns raised by the parent. ✔ Add to the plan as needed.

FOURTH ACTIVITY: EXPLORE POTENTIAL BARRIERS

Anticipate and explore factors that might get in the way of successful implementation, proactively working with the parent to identify potential barriers before the plan is put into motion. The counselor wants to confirm a plan that the parent finds reasonable and feels will help the student. A plan without parent support is unlikely to succeed.

PHONE SCRIPT: EXPLORING BARRIERS	NOTES FOR THE EHC COUNSELOR
I'm glad you feel positive about the plan. Your opinion is really important. *No plan is foolproof. Let's talk about what might get in the way, because we want this to work.* *From your perspective, are there any barriers that could stand in the way of Lee's plan working for her?* *Optional:* *[What might keep Lee from trying this?* *What might be hard for you?* *Which parts of the plan do you feel good about and think might help?]* *Examples of ways to address barriers:* *Lee said you might be concerned about transportation. The school has a bus that drops students at their homes after the homework club. Would you be comfortable with Lee riding that bus? Or is there someone who could pick her up from school?* *You mentioned that she does not wake up to her cell phone alarm. Would you be willing to help her get up on time?*	✔ Consider possible barriers before finalizing a plan. ✔ Normalize that everyone faces barriers. ✔ Brainstorm ideas to address any barriers or challenges identified by the parent.

FIFTH ACTIVITY: FINALIZE THE SUPPORT PLAN

PHONE SCRIPT: FINALIZE PLAN	NOTES FOR THE EHC COUNSELOR
I want to make sure we are both on the same page. Let's review what is on the plan, who will do which parts, and when they will happen. Example: *I will send you the information tomorrow about signing up for the home-work club. You said you are willing to call the school by the end of the week to get Lee signed up. Lee has already agreed to go to the club once she is signed up.*	✔ Summarize final plan. ✔ Review next steps to begin implementing the plan, including the who, what, and when.

SIXTH ACTIVITY: INCREASE MOTIVATION WHEN NEEDED

The counselor aims to end the call with the parent feeling positive about the plan. Some parents will be enthusiastic and ready to act. Others may be hesitant. Some of the behavior change strategies for reluctant students could also be helpful with parents. The following list is intended as a menu of possible strategies, not as a checklist to use with every reluctant parent.

STRATEGY: CHECK ON OWNERSHIP OF THE PLAN.

- *Do we have a plan that you feel good about?*
- *What would you add or take out so you could feel good about the plan?*

STRATEGY: RATE PARENT'S CONFIDENCE IN THE PLAN.

- *On a scale of 1 to 10, where 1 is not confident and 10 is very confident, how confident are you that the plan we have discussed will be helpful?*

Not confident								Very confident	
1	2	3	4	5	6	7	8	9	10

- *Why did you rate your confidence at 5?*

- *What would make it higher?*

- *What would have to happen to move the number up a notch?*

STRATEGY: EXPLORE HESITANCY WITHOUT RATING.

- *What would help you feel ready to try the plan?*

- *You are thinking that your daughter might not need help right now. How would you know that it was time to do something about her distress?*

- *You seem hesitant. Let's think how we can rework the plan to make it fit better for you and your son.*

SEVENTH ACTIVITY: END THE PHONE CALL

The counselor ends the call by:

- Thanking the parent for his or her time, insights, and commitment.

- Expressing confidence in the plan, restating that many students are stressed during the transition to middle school, and students with similar plans have been very successful managing their distress.

- Communicating that the counselor will mail or e-mail a copy of the plan to the parent.

- Encouraging the parent to check in with the student regularly about how things are going in general and specifically about whether or not the plan is helping.

- Letting the parent know to expect another call in two to three weeks.

The Second Parent Phone Call

The EHC counselor calls the parent two to three weeks after the first call to inquire about the plan and monitor progress. During this second call, the counselor and parent have the opportunity to discuss what is working and what is not.

When we talked a few weeks ago, we discussed a plan to support Lee [restate specific plan]. *I'm calling to see how things are going, what happened with the plan, and if you ran into any problems setting things up.* [*How are things going for Lee? How are you feeling about the plan? Have you had any problems implementing the plan?*]

If the plan has been implemented and seems to be working well, the counselor reinforces successes and checks on any additional needs.

That's great. Is there anything else you think would be helpful for Lee right now?

If only part of the plan has been implemented, or if there has been no reduction in the student's distress, the counselor reflects and gathers information.

It sounds like this plan has been hard to pull together. Have you run into any particular barriers? I wonder if you are rethinking whether the plan will work and have other ideas about how to get support for Lee.

If the parent has run into barriers, the counselor can ask the parent for suggestions and brainstorm ideas to get the plan going. It may be helpful to refer to the first phone conversation to review ideas that were discussed earlier. Parents sometimes need different referral options or need to get others involved to assist with implementation of a plan.

The counselor wants to leave the parent feeling supported, encouraged, and motivated. To end the second call, the counselor again thanks the parent, summarizes the conversation, and expresses confidence. Parents are reassured that change takes time.

Handling Special Circumstances

PARENTS WHO DON'T SPEAK ENGLISH

During the Check-In, the student identifies a parent or guardian for the counselor to call. Sometimes the only person to call speaks limited or no English. Schools use a variety of approaches to communicate with non-English-speaking caregivers. It may be possible to work with a bilingual staff person or access translators employed by the school or district. A language line where users pay by the minute may also be a possibility for making the connection. Students may suggest another adult who can help translate for the parent on a three-way line or speakerphone. It is not a good idea to use the student or a nonadult sibling as the translator. When no options for verbal communication are available, the counselor may choose to write a message and have it translated into the parent's first language.

STUDENTS WHO LIVE IN MULTIPLE HOUSEHOLDS

Many students live in two households. During the Check-In, the EHC counselor and the student discuss the logistics of phone calls to multiple households. Whenever possible, the counselor will make calls to both households, but will honor student requests to call only one household.

CONCERNS ABOUT ABUSE OR RISK OF SELF-HARM

The Student Check-In does not directly ask students about suicide or child abuse. On very rare occasions, information surfaces during the Student Check-In that warrants an exceptional response to ensure the student's safety. Reports of suicidal thoughts or actions or of physical or sexual abuse require the EHC counselor to break confidentiality and disclose information in service of the student's safety.

The EHC team, like other health and education professionals, operates under a standard known as Duty to Warn. This means that they must follow legal and ethical guidelines to take reasonable precautions to protect students from violent or other harmful behavior. Schools have policies and procedures in place that comply with the Duty to Warn, and the EHC team will follow these guidelines. The team member who hears about any risk of harm will communicate directly with the student and parent and will tie in with the necessary school administrators to determine the best course of action.

When a student's concern surfaces during the Check-In, the counselor waits until the end of the interview to address it. This allows the counselor to continue to gather information that may relate specifically to the risk and inform a safety plan or Support Plan. The following examples illustrate how the

EHC counselor handles communications with students. The counselor addresses the concern directly, reminding the student about the discussion of safety at the start of the Check-In:

Remember that I told you when we started today that there are times when I need to share information with others in order to keep everyone safe? This is one of the situations I told you about. I am concerned that you may not be safe, so I will need to talk your parent, and together we will make a safety plan.

Then the counselor might reflect back to the student about the information that raised a concern.

- *When you say that you have no reason to go on, I am concerned that you might hurt yourself.*
- *You mentioned that you seem to be feeling pretty upset about failing math and what that will mean. You seem scared, so I am going to ask you a few more questions just to make sure you are safe.*
- *You indicated that in the past you were abused by your uncle. I'm going to talk the situation over with your parent to make sure that you and your siblings are currently safe.*
- *What you are sharing with me makes me believe that this person may do something to hurt your friend. I really want everyone to be safe. I am going to need to share this information with other adults. Let's talk this through before I take action so that you know exactly what will happen next.*

After the discussion with the student, the counselor follows school protocol and at some point notifies appropriate school staff. It is important to be honest with the student about what will happen in the process, who is involved, and what part the ECH counselor will play. Most school protocols will include the parent in the process unless there is a concern that the parent will harm the student.

The counselor addresses concerns with the parent toward the beginning of the parent phone call and afterward reviews the overall plan. The counselor responds to any questions the parent may have and obtains the parent's support for a specific plan for addressing risk of harm to the student.

Example in the case of risk of self-harm:

I am concerned because John seems to be feeling pretty stressed right now and says he sometimes thinks about hurting himself as a way to handle his stress. We know that many adolescents his age think about suicide even though few actually harm themselves, but we need to make sure they have safe ways to handle problems. John and I agreed that it might be helpful for him to get professional support so that he does not attempt to take his own life.

Examples in the case of suspected abuse:

- *I was concerned because Jane talked to me about being touched in her private parts by another student. Are you aware that she had this experience?*
- *Ben told me that he got the bruise on his face when his brother's friend hit him. He says he is pretty scared, and I'm concerned about his safety. Could we talk about what you know about it? I may need to make a report.*

Once the EHC counselor has related information to the parent about the student's experience of abuse or risk of self-harm, she will work with school administrators and parents to determine if a report should be made to child protective services or to the police.

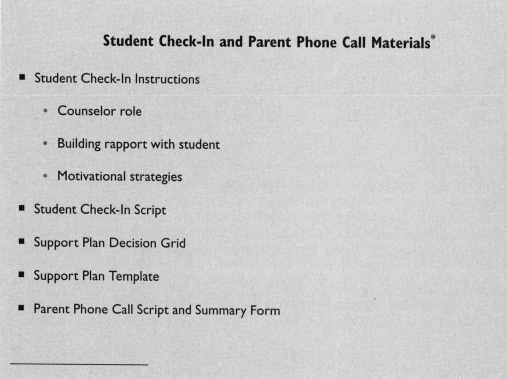

Student Check-In and Parent Phone Call Materials*

- Student Check-In Instructions

  - Counselor role

  - Building rapport with student

  - Motivational strategies

- Student Check-In Script

- Support Plan Decision Grid

- Support Plan Template

- Parent Phone Call Script and Summary Form

---

* These materials are in Appendix C.

Chapter 12

Wrapping Up

The Annual EHC Program Review

After the parent phone calls are completed, it is time for the program coordinator to take stock of EHC implementation, do a thorough review, and report back to the school community. The annual EHC program review is the foundation for decision making about program implementation in future years. The program review has two sources of information. The first source is the data collected by the EHC team. In each successive part of the EHC, the team systematically documents participation and outcomes. The program coordinator compiles and analyzes these data. Most stakeholders will want answers to the questions listed below. There may be additional questions that are pertinent to a specific community.

1. EHC PARTICIPATION RATES

- How many students participated on Screening Day, opted out of participation, or did not bring back the parent permission form?

- How did participation rates differ by race, ethnicity, gender, and specific school population (e.g., special education enrollees, English language learners)?

- How did participation rates differ by school, if the EHC was implemented in multiple settings?

2. SCREENING RESULTS

- How many students screened positive and had a Student Check-In?

- How did students who screened positive differ from students who screened negative in features such as race, ethnicity, gender, and specific school populations (e.g., special education enrollees, English language learners)?

- How did the percentage of students screening positive differ by school, if the program was implemented in multiple schools?

3. OUTCOMES OF THE STUDENT CHECK-INS

- Who needed a Support Plan?

- How many students needed academic, social, or emotional support?

- What kinds of academic, social, and emotional needs were identified?

- What recommendations were made in Student Support Plans?

4. OUTCOMES OF THE STUDENT SUPPORT PLANS

- How many students were linked to recommended supports?

- What were the barriers for students who were not successfully linked?

5. ADDITIONAL AREAS OF DATA COLLECTION

- How many translators were used?

- What languages were spoken?

- What concerns or problems arose during implementation?

The second source of data is feedback. The coordinator schedules a wrap-up meeting with the EHC team to solicit feedback about their experiences and perspectives. The coordinator also requests feedback from the teachers that hosted Screening Day. Questions such as what went well, what was accomplished, and what parts of the EHC need improvement will generate ideas and anecdotes to present in the report.

The coordinator's final responsibility is to deliver the EHC report to members of the school community. Some of the data will appear in the report as numbers, percentages, and tables; other data will appear as narrative conveyed as perspectives and anecdotes. All information will be masked to maintain confidentiality and will never include names or identifiers that could be tied to a particular individual, whether it be a student, parent, school employee, or EHC team member.

Wrapping up the EHC each year includes informing, thanking, and hearing from as many community members as possible. Written or oral summaries of the annual report are shared with the principal and key administrative staff and might be presented at school-wide staff meetings, parent forums, or district-wide events. Reporting EHC implementation results to the school community serves dual purposes. It is a chance to inform the community about how the program went and, at the same time, learn about the perspectives of community members and hear their recommendations.

Tailoring the EHC to Fit Other Community Needs

The basic EHC model can be modified to use in a variety of circumstances. Champions who are invested in improving the emotional health of students in the school setting may decide to adapt the program to address concerns that are unique to their community. The EHC might be employed to target a different population, a different emotional health problem, or a different transition. The EHC could be implemented as a response to community trauma, when a single tragic event, such as a suicide, shooting, or natural disaster, shakes an entire community. Adaptations to the basic EHC model should be made with consultation from mental health experts.

DIFFERENT TARGET POPULATION

The EHC program was designed to be implemented at the universal level, meaning that it targets all students transitioning to middle school, regardless of their known risk status for emotional health problems. However, the EHC could be implemented at a targeted level. A targeted EHC program would be offered to only a subset of students. For example, a school might decide to screen only students who are in a high-risk group, such as students who have failed one or more courses in sixth grade, students who are new to the country, or students with poor attendance. A district with marked disparities in risk status of students enrolled in different schools may decide to target only high-risk middle schools.

DIFFERENT EMOTIONAL HEALTH TARGET

A school or district may be more concerned about a different emotional health problem than about general emotional distress. The EHC procedures for screening, follow-up assessments, and tying in with parents could be applied to other difficult-to-detect emotional health problems. The main adaptation would be to use a validated questionnaire that can accurately identify the targeted concern.

SCREENING FOR ANXIETY

Some communities are very concerned about student anxiety. Anxiety may be prevalent for any number of reasons. For example, some schools have many students whose anxiety is caused by high academic pressure (Luthar, 2003), while others have high levels because their school is located in a neighborhood with a high crime rate (Vine et al., 2012). Schools that decide to screen for anxiety could use the Screen for Child Anxiety-Related Disorders (SCARED) questionnaire (Birmaher, Khetarpal, Cully, Brent, & McKenzie, 1995). The SCARED is a measure with 41 items that has been validated with children and adolescents from different racial backgrounds (Birmaher et al., 1999; Boyd, Ginsbert, Lambert, Cooley, & Campbell, 2003; Hale, Crocetti, Raaijmakers & Meeus, 2011).

SCREENING FOR SUICIDE RISK

The EHC has the capacity to screen for suicide risk, but not to implement timely follow-up to address students with acute risk. The original MFQ has 33 items, including three items about suicidal and morbid thoughts: "I thought about killing myself"; "I thought about death and dying"; and "I thought that life was not worth living" (Angold & Costello, 1987). When the EHC was under development, a decision was made to exclude these items from the distress screen. The rationale was that if a student had endorsed one or more of these items, it would reflect a higher and more acute level of need than the screening team could address in a timely manner. A school with the mental health resources to immediately follow up with a large number of students who endorsed one or more of the MFQ suicide items on Screening Day could use the EHC for suicide screening.

SCREENING FOR CLINICAL DEPRESSION

At the recommendation of the U.S. Preventive Services Task Force (USPSTF; 2009), many primary health care settings routinely screen 12–18-year-old adolescents for major depression during outpatient visits. They use screening tools such as the adolescent version of the nine-item Patient Health Questionnaire (PHQ-A) depression scale (Kroencke, Spitzer, & Williams, 2001; Johnson, Harris, Spitzer, & Williams, 2002). The USPSTF emphasizes that primary health care clinics should carry out routine depression screening only when systems are in place to ensure accurate diagnosis and effective treatment and follow-up (Williams, O'Connor, Eder, & Whitlock, 2009). Increasingly, schools have on-site mental health experts or collaborative arrangements with community mental health providers. A school that has these resources might decide to use the PHQ-A to screen for major depression. The PHQ-A is not an appropriate tool to screen for general distress.

DIFFERENT TRANSITIONS

The Student Check-In incorporates broad principles of collaboration, empowerment, and problem solving, all of which apply in providing emotional health support to people across a wide age range and facing a variety of challenges. The EHC could be adapted for use at developmental transitions other than the transition to middle school. Research conducted in Chicago reported that 80% of eventual dropouts could be identified on the basis of how well they did in ninth grade (Neild & Balfanz, 2006). Therefore, the transition from middle to high school is another time when it is critical for students to get off to a healthy start. The EHC could be implemented at the transition to high school utilizing the MFQ, which is valid for use with adolescents through the age of 17.

There are a number of adaptations that could be made to the EHC for high school students. With consultation from mental health counselors who work with high school students, the ECH team could adapt the EHC scripts to better fit the concerns and vocabulary of older adolescents. The EHC resource list would include a broader range of community resources to take into account the greater mobility and independence of high school students. A word of warning: As adolescents get older, more will score in the range of 18 and above on the MFQ. Whereas 15% of middle school students score in this range, high schools can expect a higher percentage of students, particularly females, to score above the middle school cutoff score (Hankin, Abramson, Moffitt, Silva, McGee & Angel, 1998).

Another transition to consider would be when students transfer into a school over the course of the school year. The screening part of the EHC could be administered to students on an individual rather than a classroom basis at the time they enrolled at their new school. Student Check-Ins and Parent Phone Calls would follow the EHC protocol with minor adaptation of scripts.

DIFFERENT CIRCUMSTANCES

School tragedies are in the news every day. School shootings, suicides, fatal motor vehicle crashes, and all manner of natural disasters befall our communities and leave in their wake widespread distress. Agencies such as FEMA, public health, police and fire departments, and local organizations respond with support. When communities experience trauma, schools can take an active approach to support distressed students. A school could mobilize quickly to implement the EHC as a way to identify children who are most vulnerable to the stressor and provide them with extra emotional support.

A measure called the UCLA Stress Reaction Index (Steinberg, Brymer, Decker, & Pynoos, 2004) is used to screen youths ages 7–17 years for post-traumatic stress disorder (PTSD), a specific type of anxiety. This PTSD screening tool has 46 items and has been administered to adolescents in the classroom setting (Mbwayo et al., 2015). It is well suited for communities struggling in the wake of major events such as natural disasters, terrorist attacks, or community-wide violence (Balaban et al., 2005). The EHC could shift its focus to detection of PTSD and shift the focus of Screening Day to serve as a triage system for connecting distressed students to counselors and other community members with postdisaster mental health intervention training. As with other adaptations, implementing the EHC with a focus on trauma would require collaboration with mental health experts.

DIFFERENT PURPOSE

The EHC has been used to find students who could benefit from specific intervention programs offered at schools. One program, Positive Thoughts and Actions, used the EHC to determine the eligibility of seventh grade students to participate in a group-based cognitive-behavioral preventive intervention (McCarty, Violette, Duong, Cruz, & McCauley, 2013). The High School Transition Program used the EHC to identify eighth grade students who were appropriate for a group cognitive-behavioral therapy intervention (McCauley, Vander Stoep, & Pelton, 2004).

Wrapping It Up

The EHC team has a lengthy to-do list:

- Prepare the school community to implement the EHC.

- Inform parents and students.

- Organize parent permission.

- Administer and score questionnaires.

- Check in with students who screen positive for distress.

- Create a plan with each student in need of support.

- Connect with parents to confirm and enact the plan.

- Compile information and report to the school community.

When the EHC is concluded for the year, it is worthwhile for the EHC team members and members of the school community to look back and appreciate what has been accomplished. The EHC team has completed a big job that has involved the entire school community. If all goes according to plan:

- Teachers and administrators have increased their awareness about stress as it relates to the transition to middle school and are appreciative that distressed students have been linked to helpful resources.

- Special services staff are relieved that the school has increased the on-site presence of adults who are attending to the emotional health needs of distressed students.

- Parents have connected with school staff and developed a positive attitude about their child's new school.

- Students are glad to see friends who are distressed receive a helping hand.

- Students who have been helped with linkage to simple supports feel more competent, confident, and connected within the new middle school setting.

Time to imagine. It is almost October. Is this the year for your school to try out the Emotional Health Checkup?

Appendix A

Orientation and Training Materials

Program Coordinator Task List

The program coordinator mobilizes, motivates, trains, and supervises the EHC team and stays in communication with the principal, teachers, and other members of the school community. The coordinator task list and sample materials are below.

TASK LIST	RESOURCES IN APPENDIX A
■ Orient school community to EHC	✔ Agenda for Community Orientation ✔ EHC Handout for School Community and EHC Staff ✔ Importance of Maintaining Confidentiality Handout
■ Recruit the EHC team ■ Provide general training ■ Provide specialized screening training ■ Provide specialized EHC counselor training	✔ Agenda for General EHC Team Training ✔ EHC Handout for School Community and EHC Staff ✔ General Team Training PowerPoint ✔ Importance of Maintaining Confidentiality Handout ✔ Training Agenda: Screening Team ✔ Training Agenda: EHC Counselors ✔ EHC Counselor Observation Checklist
■ Catalog school and community resources	✔ Sample Resource Brochure
■ Provide supervision to the team ■ Monitor implementation activities	✔ Supervision and Monitoring Tips
■ Conduct an annual EHC program review ■ Report to the school community	✔ Annual EHC Report ✔ EHC Report PowerPoint Template

Tips for Supervision and Monitoring

SCREENING TEAM

- Be on-site at school to coach teams throughout screening day.

- Make notes about strengths and weaknesses.

- Debrief with team at breaks or lunch to improve performance, as needed.

- Schedule a review meeting after screening day to review screening day implementation, including recommendations for future training and classroom screening implementation.

EHC COUNSELORS

- New counselors observe a student check-in conducted by the supervisor or experienced EHC counselor.

- Supervisor observes a student check-in by each new EHC counselor to provide coaching in session.

- New counselors observe a parent phone call conducted by the supervisor or experienced EHC counselor.

- Observe a parent phone call by each new EHC counselor to provide coaching.

- Meet with EHC counselors at end of each day to debrief student check-ins and to become aware of any concerns or follow-up needed.

- Schedule a review meeting after check-ins are completed to evaluate the student check-in process, including recommendations for future training and check-in implementation.

School Community Orientation Agenda

- What is the Emotional Health Checkup?
  - *EHC goals*
  - *EHC procedures*

- Why offer students an Emotional Health Checkup as they start middle school?

- How can teachers and school staff support the EHC?

- Importance of maintaining confidentiality.

- Commonly asked questions about the EHC.

- Question-and-answer time.

Emotional Health Checkup Handout

What is the emotional health checkup?

- The Emotional Health Checkup (EHC) is a program that is offered to all students who are entering their first year of middle school.

- The goals of the EHC are to identify and address student distress.

- Students who participate in the EHC complete a brief questionnaire that detects signs of distress.

- Students who show signs of distress on their questionnaire meet one-on-one at school with an EHC counselor.

- In the brief meeting, the student and EHC counselor determine the source of the student's distress and the resources the student has to cope with distress.

- If there is a need for additional support in areas of academic, social, or emotional health, the student and the EHC counselor draft a support plan.

- The EHC counselor calls the student's parent or guardian on the phone, and together they help the student get linked to support.

- Students are linked to available resources, like homework clubs, after-school activities, a school counselor, or other supports that can help them get off to a healthy start in middle school.

- All students are encouraged to get an Emotional Health Checkup.

- Parent permission is required.

- The EHC is funded by. . .

Why offer students an emotional health checkup as they start middle school?

The transition to middle school involves many changes.

- Students entering middle school have a lot going on. They typically leave small neighborhood elementary schools and move to a big new building with a different school environment. They interact with a large and unfamiliar array of teachers and students. Their academic demands increase.

- At the same time, these students are going through puberty and experiencing physical and emotional changes.

- The middle school transition is a time of vulnerability when children's self-esteem, social engagement, and scholastic performance may decline.

Change is normal and exciting, but is also stressful. Distress can be hard to detect.

- Emotional distress can be hard to detect. Unlike a broken leg or a bruised elbow, it is often hidden. In middle schools with large class sizes and brief class periods, emotional distress can go unrecognized.

- Middle school is the time when there is an upsurge in the occurrence of more significant mental health problems.

- *The incidence of depression begins to increase during the middle school years.*
- *Initiation of alcohol and drug use during middle school is common.*

Too much stress can lead to distress, and distress can hurt academic performance.

- Distress can adversely affect a child's cognitive, emotional, and social development.

- Many of the features of emotional health problems (low motivation, difficulty concentrating, social isolation, disruption of sleep patterns) have a negative impact on academic performance.

- Despite the fact that we know how critical good emotional health is to a child's academic success, a very low proportion of children who suffer from emotional health problems get treatment.

- Schools are where the majority of children get help for their emotional health problems.

If we identify and support students early, we can prevent more serious problems.

- An ounce of prevention is worth a pound of cure. Detecting early signs of emotional distress and addressing distress with effective early intervention programs can reduce the likelihood that emotional health problems will persist, intensify, and become more serious mental disorders.

- Bolstering support at a critical developmental transition can lead directly to reduction in distress and indirectly to reduction in depression and improvement in academic performance.

Emotionally healthy students are more likely to experience more academic success.

- According to *Healthy Youth: An Investment in Our Nation's Future*, "School health programs can be an effective means of improving educational achievement. Young people who are hungry, ill, depressed, or injured are less likely to learn" (Centers for Disease Control and Prevention, 2003).

- Addressing a child's emotional health needs can improve academic performance (Payton, Wiessberg, Durlak, Dymnicki, Taylor, Schellinger, Pachan, 2008).

How can teachers and school staff support the emotional health checkup?

- **Encourage students to return parent permission forms.** To participate in the Emotional Health Checkup, students need parent permission. Some schools make it a homework assignment to return the permission form. Students are given a small thank-you gift for being responsible about returning the form regardless of whether the parent has said yes or no.

- **Share your classroom with the EHC team on screening day.** All of you will be engaged in the process. We give everyone a packet on screening day. Students who do not participate can do homework, read, or work on a word puzzle that we provide in the packet.

- **Excuse students who are showing signs of distress for a check-in with an Emotional Health Checkup counselor.** After screening day, we typically check in individually with about 15% of students for approximately 45–50 minutes in a private space at school.

- **Understand and respect that student information is private.** Students are told that information they share on the questionnaire or during a check-in is confidential and won't be shared with parents, teachers, or principals. This allows them to be more honest about the distress they may be experiencing. Students' honest responses are the key to getting the support they need.

Importance of Maintaining Confidentiality

INFORMATION FOR THE SCHOOL COMMUNITY AND THE EHC TEAM

Confidentiality is an essential part of the Emotional Health Checkup. Students must be able to trust that the personal information they give will not be shared with other people. When students know that the personal information they give on the screening questionnaire or during the student check-in is held in confidence, they can feel more at ease about giving honest answers about their adjustment to middle school. Only by learning about the distress students are experiencing—how they are feeling and acting, how they are getting along in the classroom and with friends, and what steps they are willing to take to feel better—can the EHC actually help students.

To build trust, the EHC team assures students' confidentiality in the classroom and during the student check-in. The EHC team:

- Informs members of the school community that student information will not be shared with teachers, principals, or family members without the student's permission.

- Explains confidentiality to parents so that they can decide if they want their child to participate in the EHC.

- Conveys to students, parents, and the school community the limits of confidentiality under circumstances where a student is at risk of harm.

To ensure confidentiality on screening day, the EHC screeners use EHC identification numbers, not student names, on questionnaires. EHC screeners take time to organize the classroom with space between students and cover sheets or privacy screens to shield answers. Screeners ask teachers to remain at their desks while students are completing questionnaires.

To ensure confidentiality during the student check-in, students are excused from class to the meeting room using a routine dismissal slip. The student and EHC counselor meet in a private room with a door that closes. All paperwork, like rating scales and plans, is kept secure with the EHC counselor. The EHC counselor uses the EHC identification number, and not the student's name or other identifying information, on all check-in forms and paperwork. The EHC counselor and student agree on what the counselor will say during the parent phone call.

Emotional Health Checkup Team Confidentiality Guidelines
Information for the EHC Team

Store all EHC information securely where students and adults cannot see it.

- Keep completed student questionnaires in possession of EHC team member at school.

- Do not post a schedule of check-ins.

- Be careful about what you write in your planners or any other locations..

- Do not leave sensitive information out on your desk.

- Do not take personal EHC materials out of the school building.

- Lock all EHC papers (logs, questionnaires, checkup notes) in a drawer when you leave school.

Carry out confidential conversations where people cannot overhear.

- If you schedule a student check-in, it should be in a private place.

- If you are discussing a check-in and must state personal information, do not mention the name of the student.

- Discussion of students should not take place with non-EHC team members.

Oath of Confidentiality for Members of the EHC Team

[This template is an example of a form that can be used during the general EHC team training to stress the importance of maintaining confidentiality during the Emotional Health Checkup.]

As a member of the Emotional Health Checkup team, I agree:

1. To safeguard the identity of the students who are taking part in the EHC from unauthorized persons and the public, so their identity will not be divulged either directly or indirectly.
2. To protect confidentiality of student information gathered on screening questionnaires and during student check-ins.
3. To refrain from disclosing the identity of individual students either directly or indirectly when talking about the EHC.

_____

Signature of EHC Team Member / Date

_____

Signature of EHC Program Coordinator / Date

General EHC Team Training Agenda

- What is the Emotional Health Checkup?
  - *EHC goals*
  - *EHC procedures*

- Why offer students an Emotional Health Checkup as they start middle school?

- How can teachers and school staff support the EHC?

- Importance of maintaining confidentiality

- EHC team roles

- When concerns arise about abuse or risk of harm

- Commonly asked questions about the EHC

- Question and answer time

GENERAL TEAM TRAINING POWERPOINT

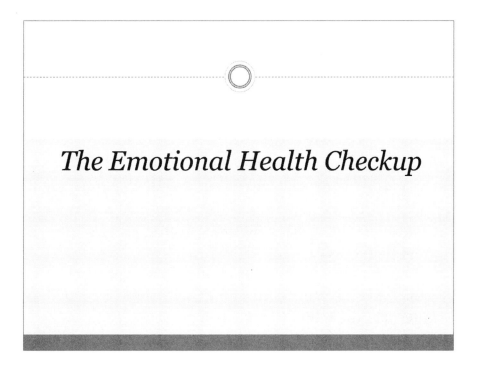

The Emotional Health Checkup

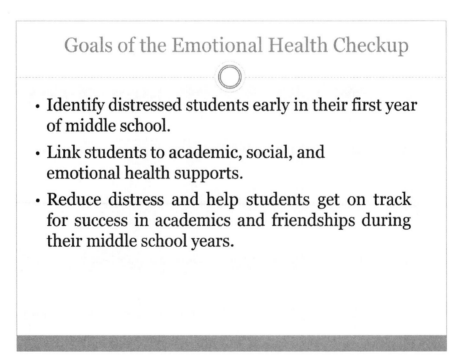

Linking Emotional Health to School Success

- Students who are distressed struggle to concentrate and keep motivated in school.

- Emotional health is a key ingredient to academic success.

- 46% of failure to complete high school has been attributed to adolescent emotional health problems.

- Early identification and support can help students stay on track.

Goals of the Emotional Health Checkup

- Identify distressed students early in their first year of middle school.
- Link students to academic, social, and emotional health supports.
- Reduce distress and help students get on track for success in academics and friendships during their middle school years.

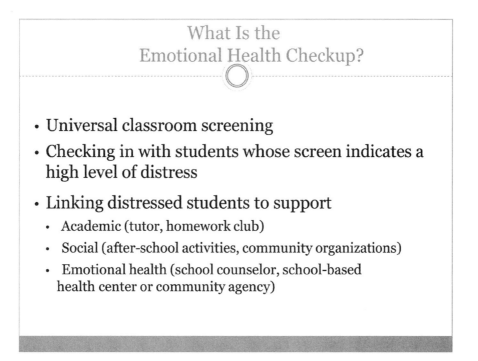

What Is the Emotional Health Checkup?

- Universal classroom screening
- Checking in with students whose screen indicates a high level of distress
- Linking distressed students to support
  - Academic (tutor, homework club)
  - Social (after-school activities, community organizations)
  - Emotional health (school counselor, school-based health center or community agency)

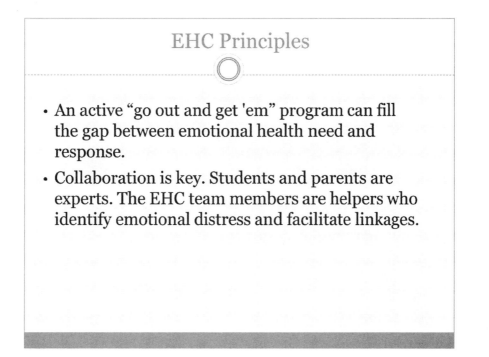

EHC Principles

- An active "go out and get 'em" program can fill the gap between emotional health need and response.
- Collaboration is key. Students and parents are experts. The EHC team members are helpers who identify emotional distress and facilitate linkages.

What Happens Prior to Classroom Screening?

- EHC coordinator meets with middle school principals.
- Principal writes letter of invitation to parents.
- Coordinator meets with sixth grade teaching team to work out classroom logistics.
- Students learn about EHC and take home parent permission forms.
- EHC team prepares student rosters and ID numbers are assigned to all sixth grade students.
- Coordinator recruits and trains EHC team.

Who Is on the EHC Team?

- EHC champion
- EHC team coordinator
- Student intro team: two per classroom
- Screening team: three per classroom
- EHC counselors

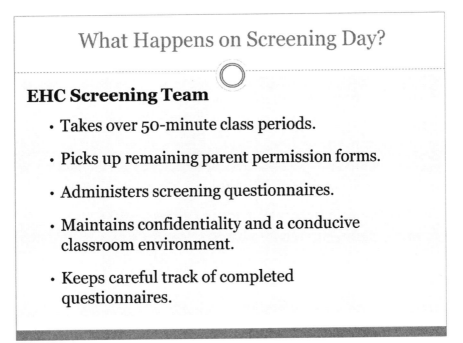

What Happens on Screening Day?

EHC Screening Team

- Takes over 50-minute class periods.

- Picks up remaining parent permission forms.

- Administers screening questionnaires.

- Maintains confidentiality and a conducive classroom environment.

- Keeps careful track of completed questionnaires.

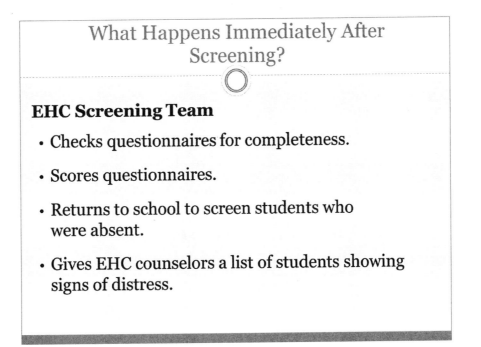

What Happens Immediately After Screening?

EHC Screening Team

- Checks questionnaires for completeness.

- Scores questionnaires.

- Returns to school to screen students who were absent.

- Gives EHC counselors a list of students showing signs of distress.

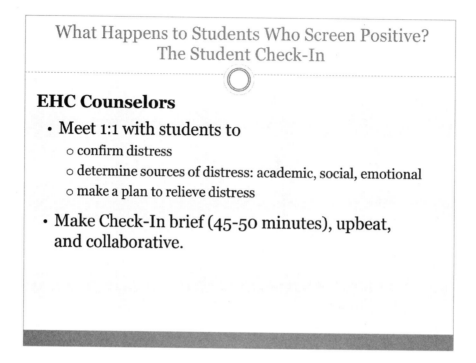

What Happens to Students Who Screen Positive?
The Student Check-In

EHC Counselors

- Meet 1:1 with students to
  - confirm distress
  - determine sources of distress: academic, social, emotional
  - make a plan to relieve distress
- Make Check-In brief (45-50 minutes), upbeat, and collaborative.

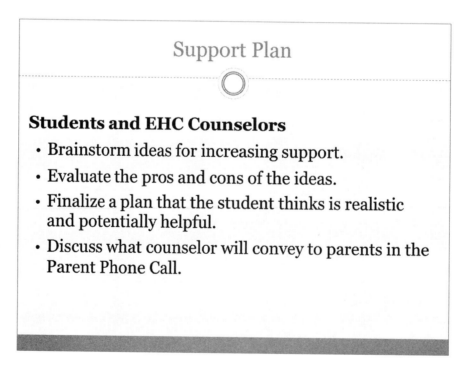

Support Plan

Students and EHC Counselors

- Brainstorm ideas for increasing support.
- Evaluate the pros and cons of the ideas.
- Finalize a plan that the student thinks is realistic and potentially helpful.
- Discuss what counselor will convey to parents in the Parent Phone Call.

Parent Phone Call

EHC Counselor

- Reminds parent about Emotional Health Checkup.
- Thanks parent for letting student participate.
- Summarizes the student's strengths and stresses.
- Solicits parent view of student middle school adjustment.
- Discusses the plan and gets parent perspective.
- Discusses possible barriers to enacting plan.
- Finalizes a realistic plan.
- Elicits parent commitment to support the plan.
- Calls parent again in 2 weeks to see how plan is progressing.

Doing the EHC Numbers

250 students who transition to middle school are screened for distress.

50 students are showing signs of emotional distress on the screening questionnaire. They meet with the EHC counselor for a Check-In.

30 students have insufficient support in place to address distress in key areas of concern: academic, social, and emotional health. Each of these 30 students builds a Support Plan.

50 parents/guardians receive a Parent Phone Call from the EHC counselor.

What's in It for Members of the Middle School Community?

- **Teachers** appreciate that students who withdraw, can't concentrate, and lose their motivation to do well in school are getting attention.

- **Counselors** appreciate that many distressed students suffer silently and that the EHC finds and helps those students.

- **Principals** appreciate that the EHC checks in with every incoming student to help them get on track for middle school success.

Tying in with the School Community

- Report to school administration, staff, teachers about EHC implementation
  - How many students participated?
  - How many students screened high for distress?
  - How many students were in need of academic, social, and emotional health support?
  - How many students were linked to support early in the school year?
- Thank community members for their help.

Screening Team Specialized Training Agenda

1. **Description of introduction process and materials**

   - *Script*
   - *How to use the master class list*
   - *Introduction to the Parent Packet*
   - *Screening roles*
   - *Lead*
   - *Organizer*
   - *Roamer*

   OBSERVE: Demonstration of introduction script
   PRACTICE: Behavioral rehearsal of introduction script in pairs with observer

2. **Description of screening process and materials**

   - *Screening schedule for the day*
   - *Script*
   - *How to use the master class list*
   - *Introduction to the Screening Packet*
     - *Face page*
     - *Questionnaire*
     - *Word puzzle*
   - *Packets for nonparticipating students*
   - *Extra packets for students who return permission forms on day of screening*

   OBSERVE: Demonstration of introduction script
   PRACTICE: Behavioral rehearsal of introduction script in pairs with observer

3. **Additional topics**

   - *Frequent questions and issues*
   - *Special circumstances*
   - *Review and question and answer time*

4. **For teams with members who are not school employees:**

- *Basic information about schools*
- *Attire*
- *Signing in as a visitor*
- *Navigating the school building*

EHC Counselor Specialized Training Agenda

1. **Review of student check-in rationale and goals**
2. **Procedures for the assessment**

- *The check-in instructions*
- *The script*
- *Use of ratings*
- *Use of clarifying questions and prompts*
- *The domains: academic, social, emotional*
- *Decision making about the support plan: using the decision grid*
- *Developing the support plan*
- *Use of the resource list*
- *Developing a menu of options*
- *Evaluating options for the plan: pros and cons*
- *Checking for barriers*
- *Addressing barriers*
- *Motivational strategies*
- *Completing the support plan template*

OBSERVE: Demonstration of check-in script
PRACTICE: Behavioral rehearsal of check-in script in pairs with observer
Mock check-in with trainer

3. **Procedures for the parent phone call**

- *Confirming the wording with the student*

- *Placing the call*

- *Documenting the call*

- *The second call*

OBSERVE: Demonstration of parent phone call
PRACTICE: Behavioral rehearsal of parent phone call in pairs with observer
Mock call with trainer

4. **Handling special circumstances**

- *Concerns about abuse or risk of harm*

- *Scheduling student check-ins and parent phone calls*

- *Review and question and answer time*

5. **For EHC counselors who are not school employees:**

- *Basic information about schools*

- *Attire*

- *Signing in as a visitor*

- *Navigating the school building*

EHC Counselor Observation Checklist

Use this checklist while observing counselors conducting student check-ins during both training and EHC implementation. Follow up with constructive feedback.

I. **CHECK-IN ASSESSMENT**

_____ 1. Introduce self as part of the EHC team.

2. Cover three areas of confidentiality:

_____ A. Remind that screening questionnaire was confidential.

_____ B. Tell about need to report risk of harm.

_____ C. Discuss call home to parent/guardian.

_____ 3. Help student feel comfortable using warm-up questions.

_____ 4. Assess academic functioning (clarifying questions as needed).

_____ 5. Assess social functioning (clarifying questions as needed).

_____ 6. Assess emotional functioning (clarifying questions as needed).

_____ 7. Ask student to identify specific family support.

_____ 8. Ask student to identify specific support at school.

_____ 9. Ask student to identify specific support in the community.

_____ 10. Assess confidence: Student rates confidence and middle school adjustment.

_____ 11. Summarize strengths (support, interpersonal skills, and coping strategies).

_____ 12. Summarize concerns.

_____ 13. Confirm impressions with student (e.g., "Did I get it right?").

II. SUPPORT PLAN

_____ 1. Develop a plan with student as a partner (if no concerns, mark NA).

_____ 2. Discuss the pros and cons of the plan.

_____ 3. Explore and address barriers.

_____ 4. Suggest wording for parent call.

_____ 5. Confirm that wording is okay with the student.

_____ 6. Thank student for participation in the EHC.

III. OBSERVER RATINGS

1. On a scale of 1 to 5, how engaged did the counselor seem in the check-in?

Disengaged				Engaged
1	2	3	4	5

2. On a scale of 1 to 5, how well did the EHC counselor provide summaries during the check-in?

Limited				Comprehensive
1	2	3	4	5

IV. COMMENTS

School Community Annual EHC Report

The Emotional Health Checkup is designed to support students during the transition from elementary to middle school, which has been shown to be a time of vulnerability that can adversely affect a child's self-esteem, social engagement, and scholastic performance.

This fall, our school implemented an Emotional Health Checkup for sixth grade students under the direction of Program Coordinator _____ and Principal _____.

AGENDA FOR ANNUAL EHC REPORT TO SCHOOL MEETING

1. Review EHC program

2. Report annual evaluation findings
   a. Significant accomplishments
   b. Annual descriptive statistics
   c. Student, parent, teacher feedback

3. Questions and answers

4. Discussion of how to make the EHC better next year

I. WHAT IS THE EMOTIONAL HEALTH CHECKUP PROGRAM?

The goal of the Emotional Health Checkup is to promote emotional health and improve academic performance for students transitioning from elementary to middle school. The EHC helps to ease students' adjustment to middle school by detecting emotional distress early in the year and linking students to tutors, school counselors, after-school activities, and mental health providers.

   a. The EHC begins with emotional health screening in classrooms. Every student with parent permission fills out a questionnaire that can detect distress in children and adolescents.

   b. All students showing signs of distress meet one-on-one with an emotional health counselor at school. They discuss the source of the distress (academic, social, emotional health) and determine whether the student might benefit from additional support to reduce distress. If support is needed, they make a student support plan.

   c. With student permission, the EHC counselor calls parents to discuss the student's adjustment to middle school and the support plan. They explore potential barriers and adjust the plan, if needed.

    d. The EHC counselor calls the parent again in two weeks to see how implementation of the plan is going and to address barriers.

II. REPORT ANNUAL EHC FINDINGS

Each year the program coordinator gathers data on how the EHC went that year. The data answer questions of:

1. Who participated in the EHC?

   a. How many incoming students started middle school in the fall?

   b. Who participated on screening day, who did not participate, and who did not bring back the parent permission form?

   c. Examine your totals to compare participation rates by sex, race, ethnicity, and special school population (e.g., special education, English language learners).

   d. Think through strategies to improve participation rates next year.

2. What were the screening results?

   a. How many students got a check-in?

   b. Examine your totals to compare check-in participation by sex, race, ethnicity, and special school population (e.g., special education, English language learners).

3. What were the outcomes of the student check-in?

   a. How many students needed a support plan?

   b. What needs were identified?

   c. What kinds of support were recommended for students?

4. How many students were successfully linked to recommended supports? (Information comes from the second parent phone call.)

   a. How many were successfully linked to academic, social, or emotional health supports?

   b. What were the barriers for students who were not successfully linked?

   c. Think about strategies to improve linkages next year.

5. Listen for or systematically elicit feedback from parents, students, teachers, and others in the school community.

6. Other information to report:

  a. How many translators were used? What languages?

  b. What concerns or problems arose during implementation?

  c. Consider other ways to make the EHC more successful.

EHC REPORT POWERPOINT TEMPLATE

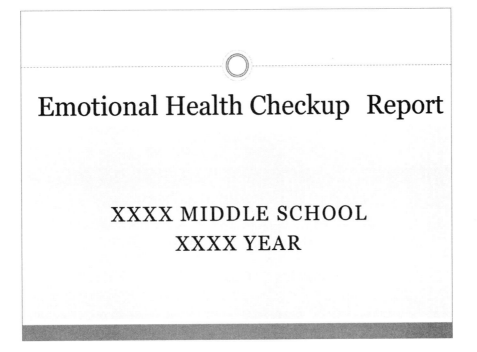

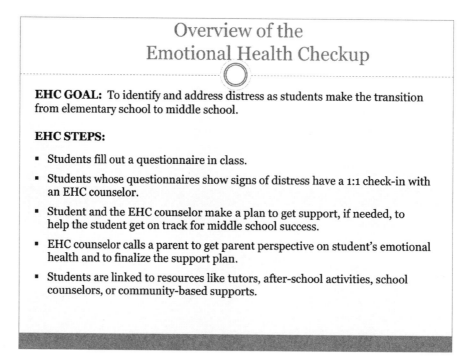

Overview of the Emotional Health Checkup

EHC GOAL: To identify and address distress as students make the transition from elementary school to middle school.

EHC STEPS:

- Students fill out a questionnaire in class.
- Students whose questionnaires show signs of distress have a 1:1 check-in with an EHC counselor.
- Student and the EHC counselor make a plan to get support, if needed, to help the student get on track for middle school success.
- EHC counselor calls a parent to get parent perspective on student's emotional health and to finalize the support plan.
- Students are linked to resources like tutors, after-school activities, school counselors, or community-based supports.

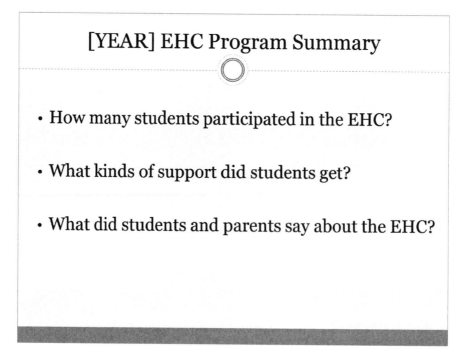

[YEAR] EHC Program Summary

- How many students participated in the EHC?

- What kinds of support did students get?

- What did students and parents say about the EHC?

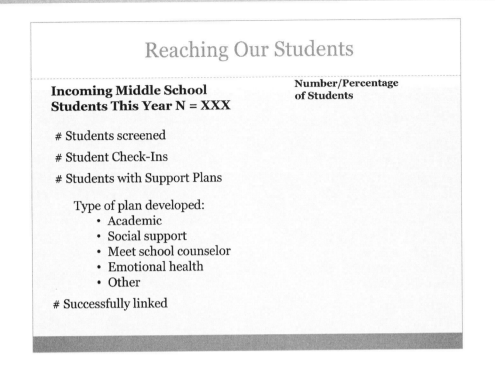

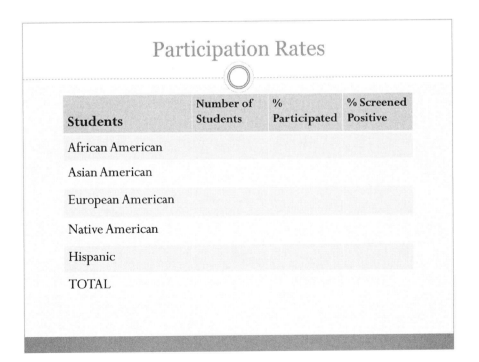

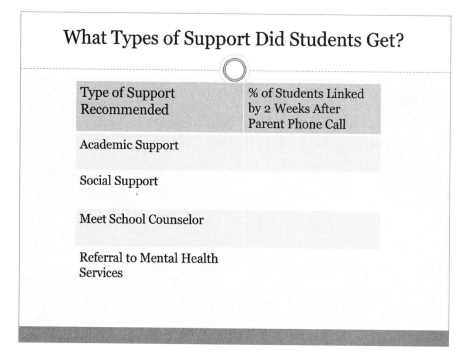

What Types of Support Did Students Get?

Type of Support Recommended	% of Students Linked by 2 Weeks After Parent Phone Call
Academic Support	
Social Support	
Meet School Counselor	
Referral to Mental Health Services	

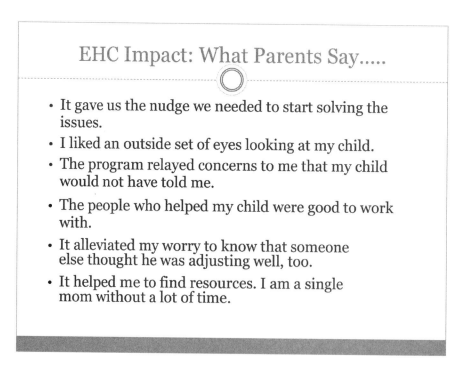

EHC Impact: What Parents Say.....

- It gave us the nudge we needed to start solving the issues.
- I liked an outside set of eyes looking at my child.
- The program relayed concerns to me that my child would not have told me.
- The people who helped my child were good to work with.
- It alleviated my worry to know that someone else thought he was adjusting well, too.
- It helped me to find resources. I am a single mom without a lot of time.

EHC Impact: What Students Say.....

- It helped me to open up.
- It helped my family as well as me.
- It helped me think about what I was doing.
- Helped me focus more.
- It was good cuz it got me into a study skill class. I am getting a "B" in language arts!
- It was helpful to know that there is always someone to talk to at school.

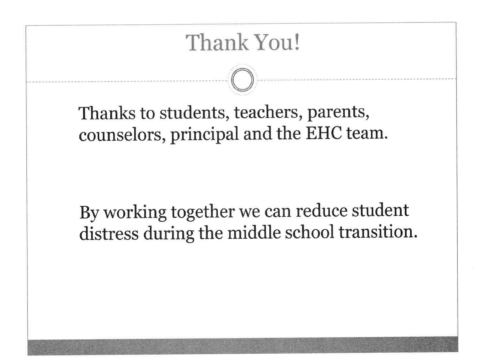

Thank You!

Thanks to students, teachers, parents, counselors, principal and the EHC team.

By working together we can reduce student distress during the middle school transition.

Sample Emotional Health Checkup Resource Brochure

CONTENTS   PAGE

Examples of listings:

ACADEMIC TUTORING

After-School Homework Club . . . . **(788) 435-XXXX**
ABC Tutoring, 222 First Street, Your Town . . . .**(608) 788-XXXX**
Southside Community Center, 333 South Street, Your Town

DIVORCE LIFELINE

- *Therapeutic support groups for adults and children going through divorce or separation.*
    Children's groups . . . .**(206) 694-XXXX**
    Adult groups . . . .**(206) 694-XXXX**

County Sexual Assault Center . . . .**(425) 226-XXXX**

Asian Counseling Services, 7200 B Street, Suite 200, Your Town . . . (507) 695-XXXX

- *Office Hours: M–F 8–5, Medical coupons*
- *Sliding fee scale*
- *Counseling, evaluations, and consultations*
- *Offer services in a variety of languages*
- *On the 222 Bus Route*

ON-SITE SCHOOL RESOURCES

School Success Counselor:
School Nurse:
Southwest Youth + Family Services:
Checkpoint Program:
At-Risk Youth Case Manager:
Drug and Alcohol Prevention Counselor:
YMCA After-School Coordinator:

Appendix B

Classroom Screening Materials

EHC Student Introduction Script

What you say is in italics.
Notes and instructions are in regular font.

Hi. I am from the Emotional Health Checkup team. I'm here to tell you about a program that we offer to all first-year middle school students in the fall. We want to learn how you are doing and how we can best support you. Today we are going to introduce you to the Emotional Health Checkup and then hand out permission forms for you to take home to your parents. We are inviting all students to participate!

We know that starting middle school means a lot of changes, and changes can be stressful. You are all starting a new school, you now have five or six teachers every day, and you probably have more homework.

[Ask questions and solicit responses to get the students interacting with the speaker.]

How many of you have more homework than you did in elementary school?

As you get older, you will find that students need to get a physical before they turn out for sports to make sure they are ready to play. The Emotional Health Checkup is like a physical, except it is for emotional health. In the checkup you fill out a questionnaire that asks about how you are feeling and getting along in middle school so far. Students who show signs of stress will have a chance to meet with a counselor who can help get them connected to support. We want every student here to have a good start to middle school.

You are probably wondering how the checkup works. We'll come into classrooms one day next week to give the questionnaire to everyone with parent permission. The questionnaire takes about 10 to 15 minutes to fill out. It is a questionnaire, not a test. Does anyone know the difference between a questionnaire and a test?

[The team is looking for answers like "there are not right or wrong answers" and "you just want our opinions." If no student comes up with the answers, the team provides them.]

When you fill out the questionnaire, your answers will be confidential. Does anyone know what confidential means?

[Solicit answers from students and then say:]

That's right. It means your answers are private. No one except our team will see your answers—not your teachers, your classmates, nor your parents.

To get an Emotional Health Checkup, you have to have written parent permission. Today we will hand out information and permission forms for you to take home to your parent or guardian. Please take responsibility for showing the form to your parents, asking them to read and sign the permission form, and bringing the form back to class with a parent signature. Your parent or guardian can say "yes," meaning they want you to have a checkup, or "no," meaning they do not want you to have a checkup.

[Optional: We have found it is fun and rewarding to give students a small gift for bringing forms back to school with a parent signature. Small gifts like gel pens, suckers, or school supplies have been motivating. We have also used a raffle to generate excitement. Every student who returns a signed permission form is entered into a raffle that takes place on Screening Day. Raffle prizes have included items such as small stuffed animals, water bottles, or candy.

We have a small gift to say thanks to each student who shows responsibility and returns a form with a parent signature.

We will enter every student who brings back a signed permission form into a raffle we will hold on Screening Day.]

Did everyone get a packet? Please raise your hand if you did not get a packet with a permission form. Does anyone have any questions?

Please take the packet home and show it to your parent. If you have a planner, write down a reminder to give the packet to your parent like it was a homework assignment, so that you won't forget. Make sure your parent fills out the permission slip and signs the form, and then you bring it back to this classroom.

We'll be back to collect the permission forms.

Your teacher has an envelope for collecting forms. We hope you will get an Emotional Health Checkup. We want to help you and your friends get a good start to middle school. Thanks for your attention. And thanks to your teacher for helping out, too.

Student Roster

Screening Class: _____   Screening Day: _____   Leader: _____

STUDENT NAME	PARENT PERMISSION			SCREENING DAY: COMPLETED MFQ			MAKEUP	NOTES
	Yes	No	No Form	Yes	No	Absent	Date	

Instructions: This is a roster for one period for one teacher. List the students and mark X in appropriate boxes.

Sample Principal Letter

Dear Parents,

Your children are taking a big step this fall. Starting middle school is exciting for students and their families, but some students will need a helping hand as they make the transition from elementary to middle school. We are excited to support our incoming students with an Emotional Health Checkup (EHC) to get every student on track for a successful school year.

The Emotional Health Checkup team will visit classrooms this fall and give all participating students a confidential questionnaire that identifies signs of stress. Students who show significant signs of stress are invited to meet with a counselor to discuss ideas for support. The counselor will call parents with feedback and work together with parents to link students to resources like homework help, after-school activities, counselors, or community-based services. Students who are supported feel less stressed. When students are less stressed, they perform better in school.

Your child needs your permission to participate in the check-up. Please take a minute to:

1. Read the Parent Fact Sheet
2. Sign the permission form
3. Return the permission form to school with your child

All students will receive a small thank-you for returning the permission form. Please return the permission form whether or not you agree to let your child participate, so that we will know that you have seen this letter. We are committed to supporting all students as they grow and develop through the middle school years. We hope you will seriously consider joining the many families who take advantage of this opportunity to help our students get a healthy start to middle school.

Please contact XXX at xxx-xxx-xxxx with any questions.

Respectfully,

The Principal

Parent Fact Sheet

Who? sixth graders

When? fall semester

What? We want to help all students get a strong start to middle school! The Emotional Health Checkup helps students who are stressed get connected to support early in the fall.

What is the purpose of the checkup?

The goal of the Emotional Health Checkup is to find out which students are stressed and then help those students get support. When students are less stressed, they do better in school. We want to get everyone on track for a successful school year.

Who participates?

We are inviting all incoming students to participate.

WE ARE ASKING YOUR PERMISSION FOR YOUR CHILD TO GET AN EMOTIONAL HEALTH CHECKUP.

If you give your child permission to participate, the following will happen:

Your child will be invited to complete a questionnaire about stress and the adjustment to middle school. The questionnaire is given during one class period and replaces regular class on that day. The questionnaire takes about 20 minutes to fill out. Participation is voluntary.

If your child's responses show signs of stress, the following will happen:

An Emotional Health Checkup counselor will meet with your child at school. Together they will discuss whether support might help (for example, homework club, after-school activities, or a talk with a school counselor). The counselor will contact you to get your perspective and to give you information about resources that could help your child with the academic, social, or emotional adjustment to middle school.

How do we keep your child's information confidential?

All student information is confidential. We do not share questionnaires with teachers, counselors, or even parents. We do not keep names on the questionnaires. They are not part of the student record. If we think your child is at risk of harm, we will let you know.

How do I get more information?

Call xxx-xxx-xxxx.

Parent Permission Form

Dear Parent/Guardian:

Please read the EHC Parent Fact Sheet and then fill out this form.

1. Print names
2. Check "YES" or "NO"
3. Sign and date the form
4. *Return the form to school with your child.* Please return the signed form whether or not you agree to let your child participate, so that we will know you had a chance to review the EHC information.

PRINT CHILD'S NAME: _____

PRINT PARENT/GUARDIAN'S NAME: _____

SIGNATURE OF PARENT/GUARDIAN: _____

DATE: _____

○ **YES**, it is OK for my child to participate in the Emotional Health Checkup.

○ **NO**, I do NOT want my child to participate in the Emotional Health Checkup.

Screening Day Script

Use the script to complete four activities:

1. Introduce the EHC and collect permission forms (10 minutes).

2. Give general instructions (10 minutes).

3. Administer the questionnaire (20 minutes).

4. Wrap up Screening Day (5 minutes).

What you say is in italics.

Notes and instructions are in regular font.

Hi, I'm _____, and this is **[introduce organizer and roamer]**. *We are on the Emotional Health Checkup team. All of you have just started middle school. As you know, there are a lot of changes that students go through at this time. Change can be stressful. Everyone gets stressed sometimes. But being really stressed for a long time can be hard. It can lead to feeling unhappy and can take the fun out of being with friends and being a middle school student. The Emotional Health Checkup is here to help you and your classmates feel less stressed. We want to make sure to give students the support they need so that each of you will have a good start to middle school.*

When we came to your class before, we talked about how students need to get a physical checkup before they turn out for sports. It is also important for students to get an Emotional Health Checkup as they face the challenges of starting middle school. The first step of the checkup is filling out a questionnaire. That is what we are doing today.

Before we begin, does anyone have a permission slip to turn in? If you do, please raise your hand.

[The roamer picks up any new permission forms. The organizer prepares screening packets for students who have just brought their forms from home and updates the student roster.]

We are inviting all students in your grade to fill out an emotional health questionnaire. The questionnaire takes about 10 to 15 minutes to complete. After we collect the questionnaires, we look at them. If your answers show us that you might be feeling stressed, a counselor from our team will check in with you in the next week to talk more about how you are doing. At that time, if you need help, we'll work together to make a plan so you can feel less stressed.

Here are some other things we want you to know about the questionnaire: We ask everyone the same questions. Also, your answers are confidential. Can anyone remember what confidential means?

[Call on students to answer the question to get them involved and keep them listening. Repeat and expand on student responses so that everyone hears the correct answer to the question. Thank students for contributing, or provide answers if no students volunteer.]

Thanks! That's right. It means that the answers you give on the questionnaire are private, and we won't share them with anyone: not your parents or your teachers or anyone else. Take a look, and you will notice that there is an ID number, not your name, on the top of the questionnaire [show]. That number is not your school ID number; it's a number we made up for each student just for the Emotional Health Checkup. The reason we use ID numbers is so that when you are finished, we can take the cover sheet off the questionnaire packet. That way your name is not on the questionnaire with your answers. No one except us will know it is your questionnaire.

You are filling out a questionnaire, not taking a test. Can anyone tell the class about the difference between a questionnaire and a test?

[Call on students to answer, or provide answers if no students volunteer.]

Thanks! Yes, you won't be graded, and the questionnaire has no right or wrong answers. We want you to give answers that are true for you.

Some of the questions may be confusing. If you don't understand something, please raise your hand, and we'll come help you. Does anyone have a question right now? Okay, we are ready to hand out the packets.

[The leader tells students how to arrange for privacy and asks students who are not completing the questionnaire for their cooperation.]

At this point, let's take a moment for you to make a private space for yourself so others won't see your answers.

[Here are some options for the leader:]

- *Since there are some extra desks, let's have you spread out to create more space for everyone.*

- *I understand your class has privacy screens, so please put one up just like you do when you are taking a test.*

- *Take out a sheet of paper, and you can use it to cover up answers while completing the questionnaire.*

- *You can use your notebooks or textbooks to make a small barrier between you and your neighbors to create a private space.*

[The organizer and roamer hand out screening packets.]

If you want to participate and don't have a permission form, you can still bring one in later and turn it in at the office. Next week we'll be giving questionnaires to students who are absent today or who bring in their permission forms later.

Everybody will get a packet today. Please keep your packet on your desk until I say to open it. There are two different kinds of packets. Students who do not have parent permission have a packet with a word puzzle, but no questionnaire. We would like you to work quietly on your word puzzle, read, or do homework so that students who are filling out the questionnaire can give thoughtful answers. Does that make sense to everybody?

[Administer the MFQ.]

For students who have parent permission and are completing the screening questionnaire, I want to show you how to fill it out before you begin. Please don't start until we've gone through all the directions. It's really important to answer these questions honestly, so please read the questions carefully, take time to think, and then answer truthfully. If you need help reading or understanding something, just raise your hand, and we will come help you. You can take as much time as you need.

Okay, if you have a questionnaire, please open it now, and find the page that says "Mood and Feelings Questionnaire" at the top. Let's read the instructions together. "This form is about how you might have been feeling or acting lately. For each question, please mark how much you have felt or acted this way in the past two weeks." This means that we are not asking how you are feeling today and not how you have felt your whole life, but how you have been feeling over the past two weeks. That means the time from **[date two weeks ago]** *until today. Is that clear?*

Again, since this is not a test, there are no right or wrong answers, you just have to mark the answer that best describes you. Think about what your life at school, at home, and with your friends has been like in the past two weeks. Remember, you are the expert.

- *If a sentence was true about you most of the time during the past two weeks, mark an X for "true."*

- *If a sentence was only sometimes true, mark an X for "sometimes."*

- *If a sentence was not true about you in the past two weeks, mark an X for "not true."*

Let's look at the first question together. Sentence number one says: "I felt miserable or unhappy." Think about yourself over the past two weeks. If you were feeling miserable or unhappy most of the time from **[date two weeks ago]** *to today, mark "true." If you were feeling miserable or unhappy some of the time, mark "sometimes." If you were not feeling miserable or unhappy in the past two weeks, mark "not true." Mark an X for the answer that is closest to how you felt. Does anyone have a question?*

If you don't want to answer a particular question, you can choose to skip it. But don't skip a question just because you don't understand it. Any time you don't understand something, raise your hand, and we can help you figure it out. Also raise your hand when you are finished. We will come by and pick up your packet, and you can work quietly until everyone is finished. You can read a book, do homework, or work on the word puzzle.

You can start now. Go ahead and read and answer all of the questions one by one to the end.

[When a student completes the MFQ, attend to the student and say:]

Thanks. I want to quickly check over your questionnaire to make sure you didn't miss any items that you didn't want to skip.

[Scan all the items. If an item is blank, the screener asks the student quietly:]

Did you mean to skip this one, or did you just miss it? It's really easy to miss a question.

It looks like everyone is done. I want to thank you all for working quietly while students filled out the question- naires. And thank you students who filled out the questionnaires. I know it took energy and I appreciate your thoughtfulness. And thank you Ms. Smith for hosting us today. We appreciate that you gave up a day of math for the Emotional Health Checkup.

[Optional: A verbal thank-you can be accompanied by a small reward, like a sticker, a snack, or a pencil. This would also be the time for a raffle, if one has been promised as part of the EHC.]

MOOD AND FEELINGS QUESTIONNAIRE

This form is about how you might have been feeling or acting lately.

For each question, please check how much you have felt or acted this way *in the past two weeks.*

If a sentence was true about you most of the time, check TRUE.
If a sentence was only sometimes true, check SOMETIMES.
If a sentence was not true about you, check NOT TRUE.

	TRUE	SOME TIMES	NOT TRUE
1. I felt miserable or unhappy...	☐	☐	☐
2. I didn't enjoy anything at all...	☐	☐	☐
3. I was less hungry than usual..	☐	☐	☐
4. I ate more than usual	☐	☐	☐
5. I felt so tired I just sat around and did nothing......................	☐	☐	☐
6. I was moving and walking more slowly than usual	☐	☐	☐
7. I was very restless...	☐	☐	☐
8. I felt I was no good anymore...	☐	☐	☐
9. I blamed myself for things that weren't my fault..................	☐	☐	☐
10. It was hard for me to make up my mind............................	☐	☐	☐
11. I felt grumpy and cross with my parents............................	☐	☐	☐
12. I felt like talking less than usual.......................................	☐	☐	☐
13. I was talking more slowly than usual.................................	☐	☐	☐

TURN OVER →

	TRUE	SOME TIMES	NOT TRUE
14. I cried a lot..	☐	☐	☐
15. I thought there was nothing good for me in the future............	☐	☐	☐
16. I thought my family was better off without me......................	☐	☐	☐
17. I didn't want to see my friends......................................	☐	☐	☐
18. I found it hard to think properly or concentrate...................	☐	☐	☐
19. I thought bad things would happen to me..........................	☐	☐	☐
20. I hated myself...	☐	☐	☐
21. I felt that I was a bad person.......................................	☐	☐	☐
22. I thought I looked ugly..	☐	☐	☐
23. I worried about aches and pains...................................	☐	☐	☐
24. I felt lonely...	☐	☐	☐
25. I thought nobody really loved me..................................	☐	☐	☐
26. I didn't have any fun at school.....................................	☐	☐	☐
27. I thought I would never be as good as other kids................	☐	☐	☐
28. I did everything wrong...	☐	☐	☐
29. I didn't sleep as well as I usually sleep...........................	☐	☐	☐
30. I slept a lot more than usual.......................................	☐	☐	☐

Tips for Screening Day

QUESTIONS STUDENTS FREQUENTLY ASK DURING THE EHC

What if I can't finish the questionnaire?
If you can't finish, then just tell one of the team members, and we'll make arrangements to catch up with you later to finish it during your homeroom. You can take as much time as you need.

Do I circle the right answer, or put an X?
Just mark an X.

What if I am between "true" and "sometimes true"?
Think about what is most true for you during the past two weeks. If a sentence was true about you most of the time during the past two weeks, mark an X for "true."

If a sentence was only sometimes true, mark an X for "sometimes."

Note to the team: It is often best to first repeat the instructions from the script.

STRATEGIES FOR ANSWERING QUESTIONS ABOUT THE QUESTIONNAIRE ITEMS

What is "restless"? (MFQ, Question 7)
Restless is when you can't sit still, when you just feel like moving all the time.

What does "cross" mean? (MFQ, Question 11)
It means you felt irritable and upset a lot.

What if I was sick last week? I didn't eat anything. (MFQ, Question 3)
Just answer the questions based on what was true for you in the past two weeks. There are lots of reasons why people might not feel like eating. We just want to know how you have been doing in the past two weeks.

You can provide vocabulary help, clarify meanings, but you should not reword the entire question. A child who is having that much difficulty should not be completing the questionnaire. Here are the steps you take if a student doesn't understand a question or word:

1. Repeat the question verbatim. Often the student just is having trouble reading the words.

2. Use a simpler word or phrase to substitute.

3. If students ask you to give an opinion about what they were thinking or feeling, say, "What is your best guess?" or "You are the expert. What does this mean to you?"

4. Don't lead a student toward an answer. For example, a student says, "I cried a few times, but not most of the time." You respond, "So what do you think best fits for you in the past two weeks: not true, sometimes true, or true?" Do not say, "So that means you fill in the *sometimes* column."

ISSUES THAT CAN ARISE DURING SCREENING

Students are sitting too closely or whispering during screening.

- You can ask students to separate themselves, or you can reseat students.

Some students are being talkative or disruptive.

- Make a general announcement asking everyone to be polite and respectful of their classmates.

- Individually remind students who are disruptive.

- Have one screener stand near the student. Often simply moving closer to the student helps.

- Ask the teacher to help with classroom management.

Screening leader forgets something on the script.

- Listen carefully as the script is read.

- While the leader is speaking, be alert to where students might misunderstand and to where the leader skips parts.

- Only interrupt the leader if he or she is getting off track; otherwise at the end you can gracefully add what was omitted.

A teacher wants to help students with their questionnaires.

Thank the teacher for wanting to help. Remind the teacher that you promised the students that their answers would be confidential. Tell the teacher it is best when teachers stay at their desk during screening and support the team from there with any classroom management concerns. They might also help by providing work for those who are not participating in the EHC or have completed their questionnaire.

Classroom Management Tips

Establish ground rules.

- Ask students to raise hands with questions.
- Ask students to stay seated during screening.
- Revisit ground rules as needed.

Keep students engaged.

- Use a positive tone of voice and a moderate pace to deliver the script in a prepared and interesting manner.
- Use questions embedded in scripts to increase involvement and hold class attention.
- Keep things moving.

Reinforce positive behavior.

- Establish a positive atmosphere using the script and a warm approach.
- Praise individual student contributions.
- Praise the group for following ground rules.

Intervene to address problem behaviors starting with minimal strategies.

- Individual reminders
  - Stand or sit near a disruptive student.
  - Use a nonverbal signal (e.g., finger to mouth for quiet).
  - Use touch or a one-word reminder of the desired behavior.
  - Voice a brief direction using "please do." *Joe, please listen.*

- Group reminders
  - State a "please do" reminder to the group. *Please raise your hands when you are finished.*
  - Refer to ground rules. *We're having trouble staying in seats.*

- Reinforce positives to the group. Ignore disruptive students and praise the group for staying seated.

Intervene with stronger strategies only when necessary.

- Deliver a "please don't" message. *Jess, please do not continue to talk to your neighbor.*
- Direct student to change seats or move away from a problem.
- Ask teacher to intervene with a student or remove him or her from class.
- Stop activity and wait for a student to follow the ground rules.

Appendix C

Student Check-In and Parent Phone Call Materials

Student Check-In Instructions

GOALS

1. Assess the student's need for academic, social, or emotional health support.

2. Develop a plan for students who need support.

3. Link student and family to support services when needed.

INITIAL STEPS

1. Obtain daily schedule and room assignment from program coordinator.

2. Be prepared with a Student Check-In packet for each student.
   a. Copy of MFQ completed by student
   b. Check-in script
   c. Support Plan Decision Grid Template
   d. Support Plan Template

CHECK-IN PROCEDURE

General: Process should be upbeat. Include positive feedback to student for participation in the EHC; acknowledge student's role as expert; normalize challenges during transition to middle school.

1. **Introduction**:
   a. Let students know that you are part of the EHC team. Let them know they are not in trouble. Invite them to participate in the Student Check-In.
   b. Set agenda using script.

2. **Review three levels of confidentiality**:
   a. **Only members of the EHC team have access to the questionnaires.** Remind students that the team has gone through questionnaires to check for students who might be feeling stressed.
   b. **Discussion during the check-in is confidential.** Review exceptions for self-harm or harm to others and the information that you will not do anything without talking with student first.

c. **Remind about what is said in the call to the parent.** As part of the EHC, you will connect with parents to thank them for letting student participate in the project and to tell them that the student missed class today. You will decide together if there is anything else to discuss with parent.

3. **Complete the assessment** following the script.

4. **Use the Decision Grid** to make a determination about the need for a Support Plan.

5. **Make a plan** when needed following guidelines and document on the Support Plan Template.

Student Check-In Script

Use these tools during the Student Check-In:

1. Use the Check-In Script and MFQ to communicate with student.
2. Make notes on the Check-In Decision Grid during the interview.
3. Complete the Support Plan as needed.

What you say is in italics.
Optional clarifying questions are in brackets.
Notes and instructions are in regular font.

INTRODUCTION

Hi. My name is **[name]** *and I am part of the Emotional Health Checkup team. First of all, I want you to know you are not in trouble! I called you from class today to talk about how things are going for you here at middle school. Remember the questionnaire you filled out the other day in class? The questionnaire gives our team an idea of who might be feeling stressed. In the next few weeks I'll be meeting with lots of students to check on how things are going for them.*

Thanks for taking the time to complete the questionnaire in class. Your questionnaire showed that you have been feeling stressed. I'm really glad to meet you so that I can hear more about how middle school is going and to sort out if there is anything we can do to support you so you feel less stressed.

I've worked with a lot of students who were stressed at the beginning of middle school, and I know there are ways to get support and feel better.

I'll need your help because you are the expert on how middle school is going for you. We can work together to make a plan in any areas where you may need or want some help. Sound okay?

CONFIDENTIALITY

Before we go further, I want to talk with you about confidentiality. Remember we said that your answers on the questionnaire were confidential or private, and that only people on the EHC team have seen the answers you gave.

I want you to know that what we talk about today will also be confidential, and I will not share what you tell me with others . . . not your teachers, not the principal, not even your parents, unless we agree on what to share. However, there are two exceptions to this.

First, I want you to know that if you tell me that you are going to hurt yourself or that someone is hurting you, I will share that information so we can make a plan to keep everyone safe. I will not do anything without talking with you first.

Second, after I meet with a student, I call the student's parent to say thank you for letting you take part in the EHC and to let your parent know that you missed a class to meet with me today. You and I will decide together if there is anything else I should talk to your parent about and what I will say.

Do you have any questions about confidentiality or what I will share with others?

ASK WARM-UP QUESTIONS

To get started, I'd like to ask you a few questions about yourself.

Whom do you live with?

How long have you lived in your current place?

How many times have you moved since first grade?

Optional:

[How old are your siblings? Do they go to school here too? How much time do you spend with your family? How much time do you spend at Dad's house? When did you move here? When did your family move from Mexico?

What do you like to do for fun?

Do you have any regular organized activities, like sports teams, band, scouts, or clubs?

Are you on a basketball team? What kind of music do you like to play?

How much time do you spend practicing? Do you attend any of the after-school activities here at school? Are there activities you might like to try now that you are in middle school?]

ASSESSMENT OF KEY AREA: ACADEMIC FUNCTIONING

ASK OPEN-ENDED QUESTIONS ABOUT ACADEMIC FUNCTIONING
Let's talk about how things are going for you in school. How has middle school been for you so far? Optional: [*What parts do you like? What parts do you dislike? Would you say you mostly like or dislike middle school so far?*]

CHECK-IN SCRIPT: STUDENT SELF-RATING OF ACADEMIC FUNCTIONING

I'd like to ask you to help me rate a few things about school. On a scale of 1 to 6, with 1 meaning no problems or good, and 6 meaning lots of problems or bad:

	No Problems					Lots of Problems
How has your attendance been?	1	2	3	4	5	6
How about the homework? Is it too much, hard to understand? Are you keeping up?	1	2	3	4	5	6
What kinds of grades do you get?	1	2	3	4	5	6
How comfortable do you feel asking teachers for help?	1	2	3	4	5	6
How often has your behavior gotten you into trouble at school?	1	2	3	4	5	6

Optional:

[*What does a 2 mean to you?*

How many days have you missed?

How often do you get in trouble in class?

Have you ever had a detention or been suspended?

What class is giving you the most trouble?

Do you have a favorite teacher?]

ASK TARGETED QUESTIONS ABOUT ACADEMIC FUNCTIONING

Ask additional questions targeted to any potential academic concerns that have surfaced. For example, only ask about homework, trouble paying attention, or detentions if identified earlier.

GIVE STUDENT A SUMMARY OF ACADEMIC FUNCTIONING

Have I got it right? Did I miss anything?

ASSESSMENT OF KEY AREA: SOCIAL FUNCTIONING

ASK OPEN-ENDED QUESTIONS ABOUT SOCIAL FUNCTIONING
Let's talk about how things are going socially now that you are in middle school. *Do you have some friends at school you feel comfortable with?* *What do you do at lunchtime? Do you have anyone to sit with?* *Do you ever get together with friends outside of school?* **Optional:** [*What do you do after school?* *What do you like to do when you have free time?* *Are you in any clubs, on a sports team, or in any other group activities?* *Would you say you have a really close friend or a best friend?* *Does your best friend go to this school with you? Is she in any of your classes?*]

ASK STUDENT TO RATE SOCIAL FUNCTIONING

Could you help me rate a few more things? On a scale of 1 to 6, with 1 being "not a problem" and 6 being "a big problem," how much are the following things a problem for you?

	No Problem					Big Problem
Other kids treating me unfairly, like teasing or bullying	1	2	3	4	5	6
Making friends	1	2	3	4	5	6
Having opportunities to do things with friends	1	2	3	4	5	6
Getting along with other kids	1	2	3	4	5	6

ASK STUDENT TO RATE SOCIAL FUNCTIONING (continued)

Optional:

[*What is the bully doing?*

Do any adults know?

What do you do when it happens?

What does a 2 mean to you?

What gets in the way of making friends?

What have you tried?

Can you tell me more about this?

Is this a new problem?]

ASK TARGETED QUESTIONS ABOUT SOCIAL FUNCTIONING

Ask additional questions targeted to any potential social concerns that have surfaced. For example, only ask about bullying only if it was identified.

GIVE STUDENT A SUMMARY OF SOCIAL FUNCTIONING

Have I got it right? Did I miss anything?

ASSESSMENT OF KEY AREA: EMOTIONAL FUNCTIONING

INTRODUCE KEY AREA OF EMOTIONAL FUNCTIONING
Thanks for sharing about school and friends. Now I want to ask you more about how you have been feeling lately, because the questionnaire you filled out on Screening Day indicated that you may be feeling down or stressed. I'd like to understand more about how you are feeling and how we can work to help you feel happier and less stressed.

REVIEW DISTRESS RATING FROM THE MOOD AND FEELINGS QUESTIONNAIRE
When you filled out the screening questionnaire in class, you said that you were often feeling* _____ .   ***Give examples from the MFQ that are prepared in advance of the check-in, such as,** *lonely or crying a lot.*

ASK TARGETED QUESTIONS ABOUT EMOTIONAL FUNCTIONING
Can you tell me how you have been feeling lately?   *Would you say that you have been feeling mostly happy or mostly sad?*   Optional: [*Do you find you have days when you feel down and days when you feel okay, or are all the days feeling like down days right now?*   *What things make you feel unhappy?*   *How would others know when you are sad?*   *What makes you happy again when you feel unhappy?*]
How about feeling annoyed, do you ever feel irritated, even at little things?   Optional: [*Do you lose your temper a lot?*   *Would you say you have a hot temper?*]
Some kids tell me they feel lonely, and I wonder if you ever feel this way.   Optional: [*How often do you feel this way?*   *Is this a change since you started middle school, or have you felt this way for a long time?*]

ASK TARGETED QUESTIONS ABOUT EMOTIONAL FUNCTIONING (continued)

Do you have trouble sleeping? Like getting to sleep, waking up in the night, or waking up too early in the morning?

Optional:

[How often do you have trouble sleeping?
How much sleep do you usually get at night?
What time do you usually go to sleep?
What time do you usually get up on school days?]

How about eating? Have you been eating more or less than usual?

Optional:

[Would your parents say they are worried about your eating habits?
Have you lost or gained weight lately?
What do you eat for breakfast?
What do you eat for lunch?]

Middle school kids can get down on themselves. Does that ever happen to you?

Optional:

[If you could, what would you change about yourself? What would you keep the same?
How would you describe your strengths and weaknesses?]

Everyone worries sometimes. What do you worry about?
On a scale of 1 to 10, how worried have you felt in the past month?

Optional:

[Is there anything going on at school that we have not talked about?
Is there anything stressing you out at home or in the community?
Does anyone else share your worries?
Does anyone else know how worried you are?]

GIVE STUDENT AN OVERALL SUMMARY

Make sure you understand how the student is functioning in academic, social, and emotional domains. Give a summary before proceeding.

Have I got it right? Did I miss anything?

ASK OPEN-ENDED QUESTIONS ABOUT SUPPORT AND CONFIDENCE

I'd like to ask you a few questions about the kind of support you are getting.
How often can you turn to your family for help when something is bothering you?
How about other adults who could help you if you needed it, like relatives, neighbors, or family friends?
How about at school? If something was bothering you, what adult at school could you turn to for help?
In the last year, have you seen someone like a counselor, doctor, or maybe a person at your place of worship because you were feeling stressed?

Optional:

[Who in the family would you turn to first? Who else could you go to in the family?
Are you still getting support from this counselor? How often?
Is it easy to get time with the people who support you when you want someone to talk with?]

ASK STUDENT TO RATE SUPPORT AND CONFIDENCE

Check-In Script: Self-Confidence

We've been talking about the kinds of problems and stressors that can come up in middle school. I'm curious—on a scale of 1 to 10, with 1 being not confident and 10 being the most confident middle school student, how confident do you feel that you can handle your problems?

Not very confident									Very confident
1	2	3	4	5	6	7	8	9	10

And overall, I'm wondering how well you would say you are adjusting to middle school so far. On a scale of 1 to 10, where 1 is a very poor adjustment and 10 is a very good adjustment, how would you rate your adjustment?

Very poor									Very good
1	2	3	4	5	6	7	8	9	10

I'm curious—where would you like your adjustment to be on the scale of 1 to 10 in a month from now?

Very poor									Very good
1	2	3	4	5	6	7	8	9	10

TARGETED QUESTIONS ABOUT SUPPORT AND CONFIDENCE

Focus on understanding answers to the three ratings of confidence elicited above.

Optional:

[*So you are at a 6 and would like to be an 8. What would things look like if you were at an 8? How can we get you from a 2 to a 5?*]

GIVE STUDENT A SUMMARY OF SUPPORT AND CONFIDENCE

Have I got it right? Did I miss anything?

NOTES: INTERPERSONAL SKILLS AND COPING STRATEGIES

Counselor notes on observations to use during decision making:
Notes about interpersonal skills:

Notes about coping strategies:

Fill out the Support Plan Decision Grid with the student and use it as a guide to determine the need for a Support Plan.

SUPPORT PLAN DECISION GRID			
AREA	MARK EACH AREA	ADEQUATE STRENGTHS AND RESOURCES IN PLACE TO ADDRESS CONCERNS?	NEED PLAN?
Academic Is there a concern? YES or NO	What is going well: What is not going well:	What supports are in place? Adequate to address concern? YES or NO	YES or NO
Social Is there a concern? YES or NO	What is going well: What is not going well:	What supports are in place? Adequate to address concern? YES or NO	YES or NO
Emotional Is there a concern? YES or NO	What is going well: What is not going well:	What supports are in place? Adequate to address concern? YES or NO	YES or NO
Other Is there a concern? YES or NO	What is going well: What is not going well:	What supports are in place? Adequate to address concern? YES or NO	YES or NO

Summarize the overall concerns and strengths and continue with either the summary script for a Support Plan or the summary script for no Support Plan.

SAMPLE SUMMARY SCRIPT FOR STUDENTS WHO DO NOT NEED A SUPPORT PLAN

Based on what you have told me, it seems that things are going well and you feel confident that, if you keep using the support you are getting from your family and teachers, you'll be on track for a good year. The fact that you have been communicating with your teachers seems to be helping. Does that match with how you see yourself, or do you think you need some additional support?

Great. Let's talk about how I can communicate that to your parent.

SAMPLE SUMMARY SCRIPT FOR STUDENTS WHO NEED A SUPPORT PLAN

Based on what you have told me, I think that things could really improve for you if you got some extra support with your schoolwork. I'm also thinking that you will be happier here in middle school if we can find ways for you to meet some kids and have fun outside class. Seems like it has been hard to talk to your teachers or your mom about your worries. Does that match how you are feeling? I have some ideas that have helped other kids in your situation. Could I share some of my ideas now?

For students who need a Support Plan introduce the plan and draft a plan using the Support Plan Template.

CHECK-IN SCRIPT: INTRODUCE THE SUPPORT PLAN

I know lots of students who have been stressed out in middle school and have gotten help to feel better. I'm meeting with many students in the next few weeks to figure out what kinds of additional support might be helpful. I think you and I should work together on a plan. A plan will give us a road map to help you get on track to do your best in middle school.

SUPPORT PLAN TEMPLATE			
AREA OF CONCERN (BLANK IF NO CONCERN)	BRAINSTORM AND DRAFT PLAN (WHAT, WHEN, WHO)	NOTES ON STRENGTHS AND PROS AND CONS	FINAL RECOMMENDATIONS AND REFERRALS
I. Academic	Ia. Ib. Ic.		
2. Social	2a. 2b. 2c.		
3. Emotional	3a. 3b. 3c.		
4. Other	4a.		

Parent Phone Call Script and Summary Form

Tools needed:

1. Student Support Plan as reference
2. Blank Parent Call Script

AGENDA FOR THE PARENT CALL

✔ Introduce self.

✔ Remind parent about the Emotional Health Checkup.

✔ Give feedback from the Student Check-In on strengths and concerns.

✔ When there is a Student Support Plan, review with parent.

✔ Solicit parent input.

✔ Confirm a plan as needed.

What you say *is in italics*. Instructions are in regular text or <u>underlined</u>.

PARENT PHONE CALL SCRIPT

Hello. My name is [name] and I am on the Emotional Health Checkup team at [name student]'s middle school. Is this a good time to talk for a few minutes about [name student] and the Emotional Health Checkup?

First, I wanted to remind you that the EHC is a program at [name] Middle School that involves all students during the transition to middle school and is designed to help students who are stressed. We know that starting middle school can be stressful, and the EHC program tries to give a helping hand to students who need extra support so that they can have a positive middle school experience. We find that if we can identify concerns early, we can help students get connected to supports that will reduce the chance that problems will get worse and interfere with their adjustment to middle school.

Thank you for letting [name student] participate in the program. Last week he[she] filled out the questionnaire, and the answers on the questionnaire showed some signs of stress. I met with him[her] today to talk about how things are going at school with classes and friends and how he[she] has been feeling lately. I'd like to share some feedback about what I learned and check in about how you feel the transition to middle school is going so far. Is that okay? I realize that I only had a brief amount of time with him[her] and that as his[her] parent, you are the real expert on your child.

Transcribe concerns and plan from the Student Support Plan onto the grid below.

Share feedback using the Support Plan Template used in Student Check-In.

- ✔ Share strengths and what is going well using original Student Support Plan.

- ✔ Share any concerns transcribed from Student Support Plan. If no concerns, skip and continue with script below.

- ✔ When there are concerns, share the plan transcribed from Student Support Plan. Then continue the script.

TRANSCRIBED CONCERN(S)	TRANSCRIBED PLAN DRAFTED WITH STUDENT	NOTES ON PARENT INPUT	FINAL PLAN (WHAT/WHO/WHEN)
1. Academic	1a. 1b. 1c.		
2. Social	2a. 2b. 2c.		
3. Emotional	3a. 3b. 3c.		
4. Other	4a.		

<u>Use script to solicit parent input. Use Column 3 of the grid to make notes on parent input.</u>

Does what I am sharing match how you are feeling about your child's adjustment to middle school so far? How is it going from your point of view?

<u>When there is no plan, but a parent raises a new concern, make a support plan with the parent, and note the plan on the grid</u>. This is a situation that does not arise frequently. Usually parents will implement the plan on their own with the EHC counselor acting as a source for ideas or referrals.

<u>When there is a plan, review the plan drafted with student now. Then explore barriers related to the plan. Use the grid to make notes.</u>

Options:

- *From your perspective, are there any barriers that could stand in the way of the plan working for her?*

- *What might keep your child from trying this?*

- *What might be hard for you?*

- *Which parts of the plan do you feel good about and think might help?*

<u>Based on the parent's input, finalize the plan in Column 4 of the grid</u>.

<u>Give a summary of the final Support Plan.</u>

Okay, I want to make sure we are both on the same page. Let's review what is on the plan, who will do what, and when it will happen.
Do we have a plan you feel is right for your son[daughter]?
Anything else you would like to add?

THANK AND END CALL

✔ Thank the parent for time, insights, and efforts.

✔ Express confidence in the plan, restating that many students are stressed during the transition to middle school, and students with similar plans have been very successful managing their distress.

✔ Confirm an address and tell parents that a copy of the plan and any referral information will be sent to them via mail or e-mail.

✔ Ask if it is okay to call in two to three weeks to check in on how the plan is working.

The Second Parent Phone Call

AGENDA FOR THE SECOND PARENT CALL

✔ Introduce self.

✔ Remind parent about the Emotional Health Checkup.

✔ Review Student Support Plan.

✔ Check on the status of the plan.

✔ Update the plan as needed.

Use the script to check on the status of the student and the success of the Support Plan. Have a copy of the final grid filled out during the Parent Phone Call and review the final Student Support Plan with the parent.

PHONE SCRIPT

Thanks again for participating in the EHC. As a reminder, we have been working with all students needing a helping hand.

Remind the parent about the EHC. See script for first parent call.

When we talked a few weeks ago, we discussed a plan to support your daughter. I want to see how things are going, what happened with the plan, and if you ran into any problems setting things up.

Review the plan using the grid.

How is the plan going so far?
Have you had any problems implementing the plan?

Notes

If the plan has been implemented and seems to be working well:

That's great. Is there anything you think would be helpful to add to the plan at this point?

Notes

If only part of the plan has been implemented, or if there has been no reduction in the student's distress, the counselor reflects and gathers information. Explore the need to revise the plan, find a new referral source, or problem-solve barriers.

Sounds like it's been hard to set things up. Let's talk about what got in the way and what you would like to do moving forward.

Notes

THANK AND END CALL

✔ Thank the parent for his or her time, insights, and efforts.

✔ Express confidence in the plan, restating that many students are stressed during the transition to middle school, and students with similar plans have been very successful managing their distress.

SECOND CALL SUMMARY FORM

DATE	ID			
AREA OF CONCERN	REFERRAL MADE ON FIRST CALL?	LINKAGE TO SERVICE SUCCESSFUL?	LIST ANY LINKAGES MADE	NEW REFERRALS, ADDITIONS, OR CHANGES
Academic Support	○ YES ○ NO	○ YES ○ NO		
Social Support	○ YES ○ NO	○ YES ○ NO		
Emotional Support	○ YES ○ NO	○ YES ○ NO		
Other Support	○ YES ○ NO	○ YES ○ NO		

References

Akos, P. (2002). Student perceptions of the transition from elementary to middle school. *Professional School Counseling, 5*, 339–345.

Angold, A. (n.d.). *Dear potential MFQ user* [PDF document]. Retrieved from http://devepi.mc.duke .edu/.%5Cinstruments%5CMFQ%20user.pdf

Angold, A., & Costello, E. J. (1987). Mood and Feelings Questionnaire (MFQ). Durham, NC: Developmental Epidemiology Program, Duke University.

Bailey, G., Giles, R., & Rogers, S. (2015). An investigation of the concerns of fifth graders transitioning to middle school. *Research in Middle Level Education Online, 38*(5). Retrieved from https://www.amle.org/portals/0/pdf/rmle/rmle_vol38_no5.pdf

Balaban, V. F., Steinberg, A. M., Brymer, M. J., Layne, C. M., Jones, R. T., & Fairbank, J. A. (2005). Screening and assessment for children's psychosocial needs following war and terrorism. In M. J. Freidman & A. Mikus-Kos (Eds.), *Promoting the psychosocial well-being of children following war and terrorism* (pp. 121–161). Amsterdam: IOS Press.

Balfanz, R., Herzog, L., & Mac Iver, D. J. (2007). Preventing student disengagement and keeping students on the graduation path in urban middle-grades schools: Early identification and effective interventions. *Educational Psychologist, 42*(4), 223–235.

Banh, M. K., Crane, P. K., Rhew, I., Gudmundsen, G., Vander Stoep, A., Lyon, A., & McCauley, E. (2012). Measurement equivalence across racial/ethnic groups of the Mood and Feelings Questionnaire for childhood depression. *Journal of Abnormal Child Psychology, 40*(3), 353–367.

Birmaher, B., Brent, D. A., Chiappetta, L., Bridge, J., Monga, S., & Baugher, M. (1999). Psychometric properties of the Screen for Child Anxiety Related Emotional Disorders (SCARED): A replication study. *Journal of the American Academy of Child and Adolescent Psychiatry, 38*(10), 1230–1236.

Birmaher, B., Khetarpal, S., Cully, M., Brent, D., & McKenzie, S. (1995, October). *Screen for Child Anxiety Related Emotional Disorders (SCARED)*. Pittsburgh: Western Psychiatric Institute and Clinic, University of Pittsburgh.

Boyd, R. C., Ginsburg, G. S., Lambert, S. F., Cooley, M. R., & Campbell, K. D. (2003). Screen for Child Anxiety Related Emotional Disorders (SCARED): Psychometric properties in an African-American parochial high school sample. *Journal of the American Academy of Child and Adolescent Psychiatry, 42*(10), 1188–1196.

Bradshaw, C. P., Buckley, J. A., & Ialongo, N. S. (2008). School-based service utilization among urban children with early onset educational and mental health problems: The squeaky wheel phenomenon. *School Psychology Quarterly, 23*(2), 169.

Burleson-Daviss, W., Birmaher, B., Melhem, N. A., Axelson, D. A., Michaels, S. M., & Brent, D. A. (2006). Criterion validity of the Mood and Feelings Questionnaire for depressive episodes in clinic and non-clinic subjects. *Journal of Child Psychology and Psychiatry, 47*(9), 927–934.

Carskadon, M.A. (2001). Sleep in adolescents: The perfect storm. *Pediatric Clinics of North America, 58*(3), 637-647.

Cassano, P., & Fava, M. (2002). Depression and public health: An overview. *Journal of Psychosomatic Research, 53*(4), 849–857.

CDC Foundation. (n.d.). What is public health? Retrieved from http://www.cdcfoundation.org/content/what-public-health

Chatterji, P., Caffray, C. M., Crowe, M., Freeman, L., & Jensen, P. (2004). Cost assessment of a school-based mental health screening and treatment program in New York City. *Mental Health Services Research, 6*(3), 155–166.

Cohen, S. (2004). Social relationships and health. *American Psychologist, 59*(8), 676.

Costello, E. J., & Angold, A. (1988). Scales to assess child and adolescent depression: Checklists, screens, and nets. *Journal of the American Academy of Child and Adolescent Psychiatry, 27*(6), 726–737.

Crisan, B. (2014, March 9). *Assessment of depression in children and adolescents: A critique of the Mood and Feelings Questionnaire.* Retrieved from http://www.academia.edu/6900159/Assessment_of_Depression_in_Children_and_Adolescents_A_Critique_of_the_Mood_and_Feelings_Questionnaire

Dahl, R. E. (2004). Adolescent brain development: A period of vulnerabilities and opportunities. Keynote address. *Annals of the New York Academy of Sciences, 1021*(1), 1–22.

Diamond, A. (2010). The evidence base for improving school outcomes by addressing the whole child and by addressing skills and attitudes, not just content. *Early Education and Development, 21*(5), 780–793.

Druckman, D., & Bjork, R. A. (Eds.). (1994). *Learning, remembering, believing: Enhancing human performance.* Washington, DC: National Academies Press.

Farmer, E. M., Burns, B. J., Phillips, S. D., Angold, A., & Costello, E. J. (2003). Pathways into and through mental health services for children and adolescents. *Psychiatric Services, 54*(1), 60–66.

Garland, A. F., Lau, A. S., Yeh, M., McCabe, K. M., Hough, R. L., & Landsverk, J. A. (2005). Racial and ethnic differences in utilization of mental health services among high-risk youths. *American Journal of Psychiatry, 162*(7). Retrieved from http://ajp.psychiatryonline.org/doi/abs/10.1176/appi.ajp.162.7.1336

Hale, W. W., Crocetti, E., Raaijmakers, Q. A., & Meeus, W. H. (2011). A meta-analysis of the cross-cultural psychometric properties of the Screen for Child Anxiety Related Emotional Disorders (SCARED). *Journal of Child Psychology and Psychiatry, 52*(1), 80–90.

Hankin, B.L., Abramson, L. Y., Moffitt, T.E., Silva, P.A., McGee, R.Angel, K.E. (1998). Development of depression from preadolescence to young adulthood: Emerging gender differences in a 10-year longitudinal study. *Journal of Abnormal Psychology, 107* 128-140.

Hertzman, C., & Boyce, T. (2010). How experience gets under the skin to create gradients in developmental health. *Annual Review of Public Health 31*, 329–347.

Hettema, J., Steele, J., & Miller, W. R. (2005). Motivational interviewing. *Annual Review of Clinical Psychology, 1*, 91–111.

Johnson, J. G., Harris, E. S., Spitzer, R. L., & Williams, J. B. (2002). The Patient Health Questionnaire for adolescents: Validation of an instrument for the assessment of mental disorders among adolescent primary care patients. *Journal of Adolescent Health, 30*(3), 196–204.

Katz, M., Chunlei, L., Schaer, M., Parker, K., Ottet, M. C., Epps, A., . . . Lyons, D. M. (2009). Prefrontal plasticity and stress inoculation-induced resilience. *Developmental Neuroscience, 31*, 293–299. doi:10.1159/000216540

Kent, L., Vostanis, P., & Feehan, C. (1997). Detection of major and minor depression in children and adolescents: Evaluation of the Mood and Feelings Questionnaire. *Journal of Child Psychology and Psychiatry, 38*(5), 565–573.

Kessler, R. C., Berglund, P., Demler, O., Jin, R., Merikangas, K. R., & Walters, E. E. (2005). Lifetime prevalence and age-of-onset distributions of DSM-IV disorders in the National Comorbidity Survey Replication. *Archives of General Psychiatry, 62*(6), 593–602.

Kroencke, K., Spitzer, R., & Williams, J. (2001). The PHQ-9: Validity of a brief depression severity measure [Electronic version]. *Journal of General Internal Medicine, 16*(9), 606–13.

Kuo, E., Vander Stoep, A., McCauley, E., & Kernic, M. A. (2009). Cost effectiveness of a school-based emotional health screening program. *Journal of School Health, 79*(6), 277–285.

Langer, D. A., Wood, J. J., Wood, P. A., Garland, A. F., Landsverk, J., & Hough, R. L. (2015). Mental health service use in schools and non-school-based outpatient settings: Comparing predictors of service use. *School Mental Health, 7,* 161–173.

Lewinsohn, P. M., Rohde, P., & Seeley, J. R. (1998). Major depressive disorder in older adolescents: Prevalence, risk factors, and clinical implications. *Clinical Psychology Review, 18*(7), 765–794.

Lima, N. N. R., do Nascimento, V. B., de Carvalho, S. M. F., de Abreu, L. C., Neto, M. L. R., Brasil, A. Q., . . . Reis, A. O. A. (2013). Childhood depression: A systematic review. *Neuropsychiatric Disease and Treatment, 9,* 1417.

Lupien, S. J., McEwen, B. S., Gunnar, M. R., & Heim, C. (2009). Effects of stress throughout the lifespan on the brain, behaviour and cognition. *Nature Reviews Neuroscience, 10*(6), 434–445.

Luthar, S. S. (2003). The culture of affluence: Psychological costs of material wealth. *Child Development, 74*(6), 1581–1593.

Mbwayo, A., Mathai, M., Harder, V., Nicodimus, S., Ndetei, D., & Vander Stoep, A. (2015, July). *Post-traumatic stress disorder and exposure to potentially traumatizing events among Kenyan children.* Poster presented at the International Society for Research in Child and Adolescent Psychopathology Biennial Scientific Meeting, Portland, OR.

McCarty, C. A., Violette, H. D., Duong, M. T., Cruz, R. A., & McCauley, E. (2013). A randomized trial of the positive thoughts and action program for depression among early adolescents. *Journal of Clinical Child and Adolescent Psychology, 42*(4), 554–563.

McCauley, E., Vander Stoep, A., & Pelton, J. (2004, February). *The High School Transition Study: Preliminary results of a school-based randomized controlled trial.* Presented at the 17th Annual Research Conference, A System of Care for Children's Mental Health: Expanding the Research Base, University of South Florida, Tampa.

McCormick, E., Thompson, K., Vander Stoep, A., & McCauley, E. (2009). The case for school-based depression screening: Evidence from established programs. *Report on Emotional and Behavioral Disorders in Youth,* Fall, 91–99.

Merikangas, K. R., He, J. P., Brody, D., Fisher, P. W., Bourdon, K., & Koretz, D. S. (2010). Prevalence and treatment of mental disorders among US children in the 2001–2004 NHANES. *Pediatrics, 125*(1), 75–81.

Merikangas, K. R., He, J. P., Burstein, M., Swendsen, J., Avenevoli, S., Case, B., . . . Olfson, M. (2011). Service utilization for lifetime mental disorders in US adolescents: Results of the National Comorbidity Survey–Adolescent Supplement (NCS-A). *Journal of the American Academy of Child and Adolescent Psychiatry, 50*(1), 32–45.

Mills, C., Stephan, S. H., Moore, E., Weist, M. D., Daly, B. P., & Edwards, M. (2006). The President's New Freedom Commission: Capitalizing on opportunities to advance school-based mental health services. *Clinical Child and Family Psychology Review, 9*(3–4), 149–161.

Mondimore, F. M. (2002). *Adolescent Depression: A Guide for Parents.* Baltimore, MD: Johns Hopkins University Press.

Morrison, A. S. (1992). Screening in chronic disease. *Monographs in Epidemiology and Biostatistics.* Oxford: Oxford University Press.

National Institute of Mental Health. (n.d.). *Fact sheet on stress.* Retrieved from http://www.nimh.nih.gov/health/Lpublications/stress/index.shtml

Neild, R. C., & Balfanz, R. (2006). *Unfulfilled promise: The dimensions and characteristics of Philadelphia's dropout crisis, 2000–2005.* Philadelphia: Philadelphia Youth Network.

O'Connell, M. E., Boat, T., & Warner, K. E. (Eds.). (2009). *Preventing mental, emotional, and behavioral disorders among young people: Progress and possibilities.* Washington, DC: National Academies Press.

Payton, J., Weissberg, R.P., Durlak, J.A., Dymnicki, A.B., Taylor, R.D.,Schellinger, K.B., & Pachan, M. (2008). *The positive impact of social and emotional learning for kindergarten to eighth-grade students: Findings from three scientific reviews.* Chicago, IL: Collaborative for Academic, Social, and Emotional Learning.

Roderick, M. (2003). What's happening to the boys? Early high school experiences and school outcomes among African American male adolescents in Chicago. *Urban Education, 38*(5), 538–607.

Rollnick, S., & Miller, W. R. (1995). What is Motivational Interviewing? *Behavioral and Cognitive Psychotherapy, 23,* 325–334.

Schunk, D. H. (1991). Self-efficacy and academic motivation. *Educational Psychologist, 26*(3–4), 207–231.

Smith, G. E., & Pear, T. H. (1918). *Shell shock and its lessons.* Manchester: Manchester University Press.

Steinberg, A. M., Brymer, M. J., Decker, K. B., & Pynoos, R. S. (2004). The University of California at Los Angeles Post-traumatic Stress Disorder Reaction Index. *Current Psychiatry Reports, 6*(2), 96–100.

Steinberg, L., Dahl, R., Keating, D., Kupfer, D. J., Masten, A. S., & Pine, D. S. (2006). The study of developmental psychopathology in adolescence: Integrating affective neuroscience with the study of context. In D. Cicchetti & D. Cohen (Eds.), *Developmental Psychopathology, Vol. 2: Developmental Neuroscience* (2nd ed., pp. 710–741). Hoboken, NJ: John Wiley.

U.S. Department of Education. (2011). *Schools and Staffing Survey (SASS).* National Center for Education Statistics. Retrieved from https://nces.ed.gov/surveys/sass/tables/sass1112_2013314_t1s_007.asp

U.S. Preventive Services Task Force. (2009). *Final recommendation statement: Depression in children and adolescents: Screening, March 2009.* Retrieved from http://www.uspreventiveservicestaskforce.org/Page/Document/RecommendationStatementFinal/depression-in-children-and-adolescents-screening

U.S. Public Health Service, Report of the Surgeon General's Conference on Children's Mental Health: A

National Action Agenda. Washington, DC: Department of Health and Human Services, 2000. Retrieved from http://www.ncbi.nlm.nih.gov/books/NBK44233/pdf/Bookshelf_NBK44233.pdf

Vander Stoep, A., McCauley, E., Thompson, K. A., Herting, J. R., Kuo, E. S., Stewart, D. G., . . . Kushner, S. (2005). Universal emotional health screening at the middle school transition. *Journal of Emotional and Behavioral Disorders, 13*(4), 213–223.

Vine, M., Vander Stoep, A., Bell, J., Rhew, I. C., Gudmundsen, G., & McCauley, E. (2012). Associations between household and neighborhood income and anxiety symptoms in young adolescents. *Depression and Anxiety, 29*(9), 824–832.

Vohs, K. D., & Baumeister, R. F. (Eds.). (2011). *Handbook of self-regulation: Research, theory, and applications.* New York: Guilford.

Weider, A., Mittelmann, B., Wechsler, D., Wolff, H. G., & Meixner, M. (1944). The Cornell Selectee Index: A method for quick testing of selectees for the armed forces. *Journal of the American Medical Association, 124*(4), 224–228.

Weist, M. D., Rubin, M., Moore, E., Adelsheim, S., & Wrobel, G. (2007). Mental health screening in schools. *Journal of School Health, 77*(2), 53–58.

Williams, S. B., O'Connor, E. A., Eder, M., & Whitlock, E. P. (2009). Screening for child and adolescent depression in primary care settings: A systematic evidence review for the US Preventive Services Task Force. *Pediatrics, 123*(4), e716–e735.

Index